PRAISE FOR
The ADHD-Autism Connection

"The numbers are skyrocketing—and so is the confusion. Most parents—and even many professionals—are perplexed by the overlapping syndromes, diagnostic categories, and classification schemes that are used to describe the rapidly growing population of behaviorally disordered children. In *The ADHD-Autism Connection,* Diane Kennedy provides a long-needed and very welcome guided tour of what has come to be called the autistic spectrum. A valuable contribution."

—BERNARD RIMLAND, PH.D., founder of the Autism Society of America and director of the Autism Research Institute

"As the father of a young man with autism and the president of the largest publishing company devoted to the field, I am very sensitive to new ideas that further illuminate the bounds of our challenge. Diane's book does exactly that. She clearly defines what many of us have only thought about: the link and the many similarities between ADHD and autism. Good job, Diane!"

—R. WAYNE GILPIN, president, Future Horizons, Inc.

THE ADHD AUTISM CONNECTION

THE ADHD AUTISM CONNECTION

A STEP TOWARD MORE ACCURATE DIAGNOSIS AND EFFECTIVE TREATMENT

DIANE M. KENNEDY

WITH REBECCA S. BANKS | PAUL T. ELLIOTT, M.D., & CARL DAISY, CONTRIBUTORS

WATERBROOK
PRESS

THE ADHD-AUTISM CONNECTION
PUBLISHED BY WATERBROOK PRESS
12265 Oracle Boulevard, Suite 200
Colorado Springs, Colorado 80921

This book is intended as a resource to provide a summary of current autism and ADHD research and treatments and to point the reader to the source materials that contain a more thorough treatment of the subject. None of the information presented in this book is meant to be a prescription for any kind of treatment, medical or otherwise, and reference to other organizations and materials is for convenience only and is not intended as an endorsement. No therapy should be initiated unless recommended and supervised by a qualified professional. The medical professional and the parent or guardian of the child needing treatment are responsible for weighing the risks before beginning any of the therapies described in this book. The authors assume no responsibility for inaccuracies, omissions, or errors contained in the source materials. The author and publisher are not liable for the use or misuse of information provided. The author and publisher are neither liable nor responsible to any person or entity for any loss, damage, or injury caused or alleged to be caused by the information in this book.

Details in some anecdotes and stories have been changed to protect the identities of the persons involved.

Trade Paperback ISBN 978-1-57856-498-9
eBook ISBN 978-0-307-56495-5

Published in the United States by WaterBrook Multnomah, an imprint of the Crown Publishing Group, a division of Penguin Random House LLC, New York.

Library of Congress Cataloging-in-Publication Data
Kennedy, Diane.
The ADHD-autism connection : a step toward more accurate diagnosis and effective treatment / Diane Kennedy, with Rebecca Banks.—1st ed.
p. cm.
Includes bibliographical references.
ISBN 1-57856-498-0
1. Autism. 2. Attention-deficit hyperactivity disorder. I. Banks, Rebecca. II. Title.

RC553.A88 K46 2002
616.89'82—dc21

2001055754

Printed in the United States of America
2016

15 14 13 12 11

For my sons,
Jeff, Ben, and Sam

"For I know the plans I have for you," declares the LORD,
"plans to prosper you and not to harm you,
plans to give you hope and a future."
Jeremiah 29:11

Contents

Foreword

As I talked with parents at autism conferences, it became obvious that many symptoms of ADHD overlapped with autism. When I discussed family history, I discovered that in many families there was a history of learning problems, ADHD, depression, anxiety, and obsessive-compulsive disorder. There was no question in my mind that many of these diagnostic categories have an overlap of symptoms. Diane Kennedy makes a good point that ADHD and mild autism/Asperger's may differ mainly by the degree of severity.

ADHD, dyslexia, and autism share similar problems with sensory oversensitivity. The ADHD and dyslexia cases are usually milder than the cases labeled autistic, but the sensory problems are similar. Sensitivity to sound is one of the most common problems. When I was a child, the ringing school bell hurt my ears like a dentist's drill hitting a nerve. I have difficulty screening out background noise. My ears pick up everything, and if there is too much background noise, I cannot hear what's happening in the foreground. Constant noise is very tiring for people with sensory oversensitivity. A sound that would be small to a normal person may sound like a blast to a person with autism. I know many people who cannot tolerate the sound of rain falling on a tin roof.

Sound sensitivity will often show up in the family history of people with autism. My grandmother hated fireworks and loud noises. When she was little, the sound of coal sliding down the coal chute was painful to her. An office or school environment that would not bother a normal person bombards the ADHD, autistic, or Asperger's person with sounds equivalent to a boiler factory. This very quickly causes fatigue and makes concentration impossible. I know one college student who is driven to distraction because she can see the sixty-cycle flicker of the fluorescent lights and can hear the electric wiring humming in the walls.

Tactile oversensitivity is another problem that is shared by people with autism and ADHD. Scratchy petticoats rubbed my nerve endings raw. It was like having coarse sandpaper in my underwear. As a child I could not understand why the other children and adults tolerated the scratchy wool that I could not stand.

Another trait that many people with autism share with an ADHD person is visual thinking. I think in pictures rather than in words. When I think about a new topic, pictures pop into my imagination like a series of color slides. For example, if I think about Volkswagen Beetles, I see five or six images of specific cars in rapid succession. I see the Beetle that a high school teacher owned, and I see an orange Beetle I saw in Mexico City. I can also easily get off the subject and see various beetle insects. Visual thinking is very specific because words are paired with photo-realistic pictures retrieved from memory.

Learning general concepts is difficult for people who think in pictures because all thinking moves from specific details to general concepts. Normal people form a concept first and then add details. One may ask, "How can you form the concept of what a dog is?" I did this by looking at many different pictures of dogs and finding visual elements that every dog had but that no cats, cows, or horses had. One specific element was the same kind of nose. I formed mental categories about cats in the same way. Dogs and cats can also be grouped into auditory categories of meow and bark, or they can be grouped in touch categories of silky fur versus coarse fur.

One big problem for people with autism and people with other diagnostic categories such as ADHD is learning generalizations. For example, to teach a child the concept of not running across a street without looking for traffic, one has to teach him on many different streets. Visual thinking is very specific, so the rules of traffic safety must be taught in many different places.

Diane Kennedy's book provides information that parents and professionals need to help their children. Many teaching methods that have been developed in the autism community will be useful for students labeled with ADHD. This book is an important bridge between ADHD and autism. Professionals and parents need to read literature that is outside their diagnostic categories. When they do, it will become obvious that there is a vast overlap of symptoms among many diagnostic categories.

—Temple Grandin, Ph.D.,
author of *Thinking in Pictures*

Author's Note

The aim of this book is to explore the similarities that attention deficit hyperactivity disorder (ADHD) shares with a spectrum of disorders currently known as pervasive developmental disorders. Like autism researcher Dr. Lorna Wing, I believe that these disorders do differ in clinical descriptions and degrees of impairment; however, I also agree that the population I seek to help is better served by recognizing that these disorders share similar features, especially in terms of social impairment. By viewing these as possibly related disorders, clinicians may more appropriately address the immediate needs of the patient.

For the purposes of this book, certain labels are used to describe a common set of symptoms occurring in ADHD and autism. These labels are currently accepted in each of these fields as well as in the *Diagnostic and Statistical Manual of Mental Disorders, Fourth Edition Text Revision,* 2000 (DSM-IV-TR). Because attention deficit hyperactivity disorder, combined type (ADHD, combined type) is the subtype most closely aligned with autistic spectrum disorders, I have focused exclusively upon this subtype for the discussion. Throughout the book, the generic term ADHD is used to refer to ADHD, combined type. Likewise, the term "autistic spectrum disorders" is used to refer to autism, Asperger's syndrome, pervasive developmental disorders–not otherwise specified (PDD–NOS), and high-functioning autism.

Regarding the idea that high-functioning autism and Asperger's syndrome are expressions of the same basic disorder, Diane Twachtman-Cullen believes that "given the nature of the similarities between the disorders, and in the absence of definitive information to the contrary, this would seem to be a most reasonable position."[1] Because of the similarities between ADHD and Asperger's syndrome and the absence of conclusive evidence that differentiates these disorders, an important question is raised. Is ADHD most likely part of the autistic spectrum? This book examines the issue and the immediate need for further research.

In response to those who believe that Asperger's syndrome has become the most recent in trendy diagnoses, I must point out a few things. First, Asperger's is a form of autism. It is a social-communication disorder that seriously affects the quality of life for those who have it. People often call them eccentrics or odd ducks. Yet these benign labels mask the deficits that make it difficult for these individuals to function normally. Second, people with Asperger's syndrome have extraordinary qualities that make them essential to our culture and to God's plan. Their unique genius should be celebrated, and their eccentricities should be recognized as expressions of an impairment and as an attempt to function in a world that does not understand them.

Abbreviations Used in This Book

AAP	American Academy of Pediatrics
ABA	Applied Behavior Analysis
ADHD	attention deficit hyperactivity disorder
CBCL	Child Behavior Checklist
CD	conduct disorder
CDC	Centers for Disease Control and Prevention
CHADD	Children and Adults with Attention Deficit Disorder
CPRS-R: L-ADHD	Conners' Parent Rating Scale, 1997
CTRS-R: L-ADHD	Conners' Teacher Rating Scale, 1997
DAN!	Defeat Autism Now!
DSM-IV-TR	*Diagnostic and Statistical Manual of Mental Disorders, Fourth Edition Text Revision,* 2000
FAAAS	Families of Adults Afflicted with Asperger's Syndrome
FDA	Food and Drug Administration
IDEA	Individuals with Disabilities Education Act
IEP	Individualized Education Program
IFSP	Individualized Family Service Plan
LD	learning disabilities
NIMH	National Institute of Mental Health
ODD	oppositional defiant disorder
PDD	pervasive developmental disorder(s)

Chapter 1

A Mother's Mission

What's the Big Deal About This "Connection"?

The real voyage of discovery lies not in seeking
new landscapes, but in having new eyes.
MARCEL PROUST

I live in a laboratory. My three children are walking, talking examples of the fascinating yet little-known ways that attention deficit disorders (ADHD) and autism are related.

ADHD is classified with disruptive behavior disorders in the *Diagnostic and Statistical Manual of Mental Disorders, Fourth Edition Text Revision,* 2000, which I'll refer to in these pages as the DSM-IV-TR. Although ADHD is considered the leading developmental disorder of childhood, it is the most controversial and misunderstood of all psychiatric disorders. "No mental disability this decade has been assailed by as much criticism, skepticism and flat out mockery as ADHD," said Matthew Cohen, president of Children and Adults with Attention Deficit Disorder (CHADD). Nevertheless, hundreds of thousands of children and adults are diagnosed with this disorder each year.

As for autism, researchers and physicians currently use the term "pervasive developmental disorder" (PDD) to refer to a group of related disorders that includes autism, Asperger's syndrome (also called "Asperger syndrome" or "Asperger's disorder"), and pervasive developmental disorder–not otherwise specified (PDD–NOS). These disorders are broadly categorized as pervasive developmental disorders because they manifest in a child's social, communication, and behavioral development.

It is a considerable advancement in autism awareness that Asperger's syndrome has recently been identified as a subtype of PDD. It is milder in degree than autistic disorder as defined in the DSM-IV-TR and, as you will see, shares an amazing number of similar characteristics with attention deficit hyperactivity disorder (ADHD).

What began as my desperate attempts to find help for my sons has ended up as a mission—a mission to increase awareness about the similarities between ADHD and autistic spectrum disorders, especially Asperger's syndrome, and thereby facilitate more productive dialogue, more accurate diagnoses, and more effective treatment for children affected with these conditions. My journey has been like that of a warrior with battles of ignorance raging all around me. In raising three sons with various degrees of developmental disorders, I have debated the definition and treatment of their conditions with the experts and have struggled with educators who didn't understand. As a mother, basic training wasn't optional. I had to face combat ready or not. So, armed with a mother's intuition and my Christian faith, I set out to prove something I'd come to suspect as each of my sons was diagnosed with varying degrees of ADHD: There had to be a better answer than "hyperactivity," "inattentiveness," or "impulsivity" at the root of their difficulties. These labels left too much unexplained.

Consequently, I've spent the last seven years discovering what every parent of a child with ADHD should know: ADHD and Asperger's syndrome are closely related disorders. They may even fall in the same spectrum, along with autism and pervasive developmental disorders. However, until now, no one has examined the overwhelming similarities between ADHD and Asperger's syndrome. Instead, researchers and clinicians from both ADHD and autism have focused upon the *differences* between these two disorders. I have come to believe that this focus upon the differences, to some extent, is fostered by the paradigm of isolation practiced in the scientific community. That is to say, research is a fairly isolated pursuit, and when we refer to research that takes place in two apparently unrelated fields, then the chances that these researchers have shared information are slim at best.

Nevertheless, it is my hope that the information in this book will open new areas for dialogue, research, and treatment between the fields of ADHD and autism. Even more important for parents of children with attention deficits, autism research offers a biomedical view rather than a strictly behavioral approach usually taken by ADHD specialists. With recent advances made in neurobiology, genetics, nutrition, and cognitive research, autism research presents a more complete view of what is now considered ADHD, especially in terms of causes, symptoms, diagnosis, and treatment. Current ADHD research still focuses on controlling the impulsivity, inattentiveness, and hyperactivity associated with the disorder, even though, as you will see in chapter 5, these behaviors are simply symptoms of the underlying disorder and not the disorder itself.

But I am jumping ahead. Let me begin at the beginning.

How I Encountered the Connection

My initiation to ADHD came through my middle son, Ben. Ben is truly what experts call a textbook case of ADHD, if there is such a thing. A happy but busy child, he didn't run into any trouble until the first grade when we realized he wasn't learning. The teacher insisted Ben's lack of progress was because he wasn't motivated. However, we feared retardation, because Ben couldn't hold a fork or tie his shoes even though he was six. When his school delays resulted in a diagnosis of ADHD as well as an extremely high IQ, I was momentarily relieved. After all, ADHD accounted for his delayed social and motor skills.

The relief I felt is common to many parents whose children have just received an ADHD diagnosis. I truly believed that the diagnosis would lead to answers and solutions. Instead, it led only to medication.

As is common even today, the experts recommended we treat Ben's condition with Ritalin. My husband, Tom, and I resisted this until I'd done enough research to discover there was really no other treatment option. After we gave Ritalin a try, Ben seemed to calm down almost immediately and moved into his school's advanced education program.

He still struggled with motor-skill problems and maintaining friendships, but these didn't frustrate him as much as when he wasn't on medication. So for us, Ritalin seemed a success.

During this time I came to believe much more could be done for people with ADHD, so I joined CHADD. As a parent advocate, I immersed myself in local and national conferences on ADHD and read every bit of research I could. At that time all of the literature focused upon people who exhibited hyperactivity along with inattentiveness. Soon, however, the portrait of a person with ADHD changed to reflect children more like my oldest son, Jeff, who was inattentive but not hyperactive. This newer subtype was just emerging in ADHD research.

Unlike Ben, Jeff performed well in school during his elementary years. He was by all accounts a happy, bright student. Consequently, due to our preoccupation with Ben's difficulties, my husband and I failed to see that Jeff was having more and more trouble keeping up. We reasoned that some of Jeff's difficulties stemmed from his entering middle school. We accused him of being unmotivated and lazy, unlike his brother Ben, who had a disability. It was difficult for Tom and me to see Jeff any other way at this stage. He and Ben were nearly polar opposites. Ben had always lagged behind developmentally; Jeff had always developed ahead of schedule. Where Ben had been easygoing as a baby, Jeff was much more demanding, self-sufficient, and bossy. And though Ben had his share of social troubles, Jeff made friends easily and was a natural leader. So it was hard for Tom and me to understand what was happening to Jeff.

My firstborn moved into first place for my attention when his teacher called to report Jeff was isolated, depressed, and unmotivated. In many ways he resembled the newer portrait of ADHD that had recently emerged in the research—that of learners who internalize their inattentiveness rather than acting out on it. These people tend to be dreamers who have less-defined attention deficits and who become hyperfocused and hypoactive rather than hyperactive. Jeff tested ADD with no hyperactivity, giving me another way of viewing this syndrome.

I began to consider ADHD and ADD as something like a cold virus. In one person the virus is manifested as a head cold, in another as a chest cold. This is what it seemed like with attention deficit. At first the researchers said, "It's hyperactivity—we have it figured out." And then, "No, maybe not exactly. It's also hypoactivity. Well, actually it could be both."

As a mother who had closely followed the ADHD research for five years, I thought I understood what ADHD really was, especially since I had two textbook cases of the ADHD syndrome in my home. However, I quickly discovered that my journey with ADHD had only begun. With the birth of my third son, Sam, it would soon cross over into areas of autism research.

By age three, Sam was diagnosed with severe ADHD as well as oppositional defiant disorder (ODD). The doctors told me that his ADHD was "the worst case we've ever seen," and they explained his extreme antisocial behavior was intentional and willful, hence the ODD diagnosis. To complicate matters, we were told that Sam was highly gifted with a genius IQ. Yet raising a genius with the worst case of ADHD ever seen didn't make me want to start planning for Harvard. I simply wanted Sam to be able to complete kindergarten with a measure of peace.

Where Ben's social difficulties led to his having problems making friends, Sam's behavior led to more extreme isolation. He would have numerous temper tantrums, bite other children in the back while they quietly waited in line for the rest room, disrupt class, and refuse to go to gym if he couldn't be line leader for the twelfth week in a row. And while I couldn't deny that these behaviors looked like behaviors of a strong-willed child who challenged authority, something just didn't seem to fit his diagnosis. Many times, Sam actually got along better with adults in charge than with his peers. As I examined his behavior more carefully, I concluded that Sam's tantrums weren't in response to being told what to do; they occurred in response to some change in his environment or routine.

Another characteristic I noticed about Sam was his extreme sensitivity to sensory stimuli. He never looked at me directly, and getting a kiss out of him was like negotiating a peace treaty. I never got spontaneous hugs or kisses, only "deals." Likewise, anytime I would put him into the shower he would throw an extreme fit as if he were in some sort of pain. Yet all of the ADHD research left me more confused about Sam's diagnosis. Impulsivity, hyperactivity, and inattentiveness did not begin to address the complexity of Sam's behavior. Plus the medications were having little effect on him.

At this point my intuition told me there was more to be discovered, even though the doctors assured me that Sam's ADHD was the central disorder. Yet, as a mother, I simply did not know where to look for more research to explain my son's difficulties. I continued to immerse myself in ongoing ADHD research in the hope of helping Sam.

Finally, at a national ADHD conference, I met Dr. Paul Elliott, a physician dedicated to treating individuals with ADHD and aiding their families through education. I boldly approached him with some questions about medication during a break between sessions. Specifically, I wanted to know why Ben and Jeff had responded so well to medication, whereas Sam experienced little relief. I described Sam to Dr. Elliott, who explained that the horizon of ADHD is usually broadened to subsume cases like Sam's. In other words, when a patient presents symptoms that fall to one extreme or the other in ADHD—that is, explosive and in-your-face, or silent and withdrawn—the definitions expand to compensate for these types. What has emerged from this approach are numerous subtypes of ADHD.

Around this same time, I met a mother named Joni who ran CHADD's state council and who had a particular interest in tough cases like Sam's. She had done some research on autism and urged me to do the same. *Autism?* I thought. *She must not have understood. My son is not an idiot savant. She must not have heard me say that he'd had no language delay. I pictured a child spinning or rocking, totally uncommunicative and unresponsive.* Still, she guided me to some basic facts about autism that changed forever my views of my son's diagnosis.

Joni showed me a simple checklist of behavioral problems commonly associated with autism, especially Asperger's syndrome. The checklist described my son's behavior completely, yet I would never have found this checklist in any ADHD research. Imagine my sense of urgency as I set out to track down any and every overlap between ADHD and autism. It wasn't long before I felt the relief that comes from knowing that my child and I were not alone and that he was not the "worst case ever seen." In fact, I soon discovered Sam's verbal abilities placed him at the mild end of the autistic spectrum. However, the challenge and frustrations of obtaining an accurate diagnosis for Sam paled in comparison to our experience in obtaining an ADHD diagnosis. The autism guidelines are more stringent and exacting than those of ADHD. There is also much less room for subjective opinion. Instead, autistic spectrum diagnoses rely more fully upon direct observation from clinicians.

Through Joni I met a researcher who frequently taught educators about autism. This researcher almost immediately spotted Sam's autism. Although she was not in a position to give a formal diagnosis, she encouraged me to pursue that and referred me to a more qualified coworker. I assumed the diagnosis would be a mere formality. I never imagined that someone familiar with autism would not see the symptoms in my son. Nevertheless, according to this psychologist, Sam did not meet enough criteria to be placed on the autistic spectrum. Imagine my disappointment in still not having reached a firm answer regarding Sam's condition.

To make matters worse, this physician recommended putting Sam on antipsychotic medications. These would sedate him far more than Ritalin. His reason for such extreme measures? He believed that because

Sam's IQ levels were so high, we needed an outside force to "control" or contain him in ways that would make society feel "safe."

Outraged at such fear-based and extreme measures for containing rather than treating my child, I reviewed line by line the behaviors in Sam's evaluation sheet that could be found in the volumes of literature relating to Asperger's syndrome and PDD. Refusing to be discouraged in my search for help, I persevered.

A different psychologist who had served as one of my professional advisors told me of an expert, Dr. Peter Tanguay, who had spent over twenty years researching autism and who had been the technical advisor for the movie *Rain Man.* I called him immediately. He calmly asked me why I believed my son has autism.

"Because I gave birth to Data," I blurted out, referencing Temple Grandin's comparison to an android from *Star Trek.* "I also married Spock," I exclaimed, unleashing years of frustration with a single statement. "Last night I had the same argument I've had with my husband one thousand times. He can't put himself in my shoes. He just doesn't get two-way social interaction. So I told him to get a dictionary, look up this word and then write it, memorize it, do whatever it takes to understand it."

"What was the word?" Dr. Tanguay asked.

"EMPATHY!" I nearly screamed.

Fortunately, Dr. Tanguay was in the mood to listen to a frantic, frustrated mother. He invited me to his office that very afternoon.

Tom accompanied me to the meeting for the autistic diagnostic interview, which usually lasts two hours. Ours lasted four! You see, when Dr. Tanguay would ask specific questions about Sam's behavior, Tom often replied, "I'm not so sure about him, but how did you know that about me?" Later, Tom confided in me that he had never felt so understood.

Throughout the interview, Dr. Tanguay seemed as interested in Tom as in Sam. I knew we were onto something. I'd always suspected a genetic link between Tom's and Sam's behaviors, a link that autism research bears out. At the conclusion of our interview, Dr. Tanguay diagnosed both my husband and son with Asperger's syndrome. He believed Sam's very high IQ had clouded the previous autism expert's opinions. In addition, he pointed out that Asperger's was a fairly new diagnosis and that there was a lot of controversy about how to define it clearly. Exhausted but elated, I knew we finally had the correct diagnosis for Sam and could get him the help he so needed.

I wasn't permitted to enjoy my victory for long, however. One of my closest friends, Shannon, has toddler twins, one of whom was experiencing developmental delays in language as well as temper tantrums related to changes in her environment. I began to recognize in this little girl some of the same symptoms I'd seen in both Ben and Sam. Needless to say, I urged Shannon to read about Asperger's syndrome. She told me that while she could certainly see her daughter described in the research, like Tom, she saw more of herself explained. Diagnosed with ADHD, she had been placed on Ritalin, but she knew the diagnosis and medication did not address her deeper issues. Armed with descriptions of Asperger's, however, she felt confident she'd found the missing component to understand her behavior. In an attempt to avoid this confusion for her own child, Shannon took her daughter to Dr. Tanguay. However, he concluded that her daughter was not autistic; rather, she was simply developmentally delayed.

I felt as if I'd been kicked in the stomach. All of the old familiar feelings surrounding my experiences with physicians and Sam surfaced. Then it struck me: Had Dr. Tanguay seen Sam at age two, he most likely would have missed Sam's diagnosis as well. In fact, Dr. Tanguay himself affirmed my suspicions about Shannon's daughter's age and her diagnosis. At a picnic the following week, Shannon and I happened to see him. He came over to us and wanted to clarify some issues that had bothered him about the diagnosis. He strongly agreed that Shannon's daughter had developmental delays significant enough to be considered on the autistic spectrum; however, because of the strict guidelines used to diagnose autism, she did not qualify. He voiced the same frustration that numerous other autism researchers express: It is extremely difficult to diagnose milder degrees of autism during the toddler and preschool years. Autism often manifests itself as people mature and is most easily spotted when it presents extreme social and functional difficulties for the individual.

As I talked with Shannon, some important themes became clear to me. As a mother, she already suspected that her daughter's development was not typical. After reading some literature on autism, she was convinced her daughter was on the autistic spectrum despite Dr. Tanguay's diagnosis. She also realized what many concerned mothers come to realize about their children who have ADHD or an autistic spectrum disorder—the only hope for treatment lies with the parents' ability to educate themselves about the syndromes, to seek out the best remedies, and to apply these to their children. In other words, parents of children with these syndromes often must travel alone through a maze of misdiagnoses and ineffective or inappropriate treatments.

TRAGEDIES WE CAN AVOID

As I've spoken to parents across the nation and experienced firsthand the spectrum of frustration and despair that these disorders bring, I've realized how important it is to articulate some of the tragedies so that you don't feel so alone. So often with these disorders we feel that no one understands—the experts don't understand our children, so how can they understand our pain. Indeed, these disorders breed isolation, not only in the disorders but in the tragedies that so often emerge from them.

When a mother first realizes there is something wrong with her child, the knot in her stomach does not go away. She observes intently as she engages her child, looking for a clue or a sign that maybe her instincts are wrong, maybe her child is okay. At times the child may appear to be so. But when her child fails to outgrow the tantrums, the rages, the learning difficulties, the advanced vocabulary, the speech delays, the auditory processing problems, the repetitive play, and the problems with playmates, a mother knows for certain her instincts are right.

There is something developmentally wrong with her child.

Usually it isn't until the child is in a classroom setting that a child receives the first diagnosis. A teacher might suggest that the child be screened for ADHD. Autism is not even considered. So the teacher, parents, and doctor fill out a checklist focusing primarily upon *behaviors,* and the child is diagnosed with ADHD and probably ODD. (If the child throws tantrums or acts defiantly, then a diagnosis of ODD is also given at this time; if not, then the ODD diagnosis usually occurs around puberty.)

With this diagnosis the stage is set for two primary types of treatment: chemical and behavioral. Unfortunately, these treatments are usually limited in duration, as with the stimulants, or are focused upon behavior management rather than upon the real underlying deficits in communication. And sadly, as evidenced by more than two thousand responses to the *Oprah* show's segment "Explosive Children" in February 2000, the diagnosis does not offer parents any relief in their search for treatment. Similarly, this diagnosis also sets up all sorts of negative expectations in the minds of those dealing with the child—namely that he will be difficult to handle and will be a disruption both in the classroom and at home.

Interestingly, a recent study of thirty-nine children with Asperger's, ages six to eleven, states that "by the time the diagnosis of Asperger's syndrome was made, 92 percent had carried other diagnoses or educational labels...the most frequent...was attention-deficit/hyperactivity disorder."[1]

Misdiagnosis is the number-one cause of tragedies like the following that could be avoided.

Poor Self-Image or Self-Esteem

Because of misdiagnosis, an improper understanding of autistic spectrum disorders, and ADHD's emphasis on willful defiance at the root of the problem, the adults who deal daily with these children have a tainted view of who they are and what they are capable of accomplishing. These children must interact daily with adults who are impatient with them, see them as problems, and believe they are fundamentally bad, willful children. Rather than believing that they have the support of teachers, administrators, doctors, and parents, these children often come to view them as enemies—people in their lives who tear them down instead of encouraging them. This leads children to believe that they are broken or flawed, and in turn, they begin to believe they are not part of the whole, even though this is not the case according to Scripture. This concept is reflected in 1 Corinthians 12:14-15: "Now the body is not made up of one part but of many. If the foot should say, 'Because I am not a hand, I do not belong to the body,' it would not for that reason cease to be part of the body."

Another type of tragedy touches children who try their best to conform to the wishes of the professionals and their own parents. These are the children who do everything in their power to change their behavior, who take their medicines and who try to blend in rather than be a distraction. Sadly, these children, too, come to believe they are inherently flawed, only they cope through conformity rather than disruption.

Both types of children grow into young adults who believe they don't fit in this world. What's really frightening is that as they move through adolescence, they begin to recognize that they are still sorely misunderstood and socially isolated. In those cases when such realizations are coupled with emerging bipolar disorder, this can lead to serious outcomes in young adulthood.

Unidentified Bipolar Disorder

According to *What Other Disorders Have the Same Symptoms as Attention-Deficit Hyperactivity Disorder?* as many as 25 percent of children diagnosed with attention deficit disorder may also have bipolar disorder.[2] Research bears out that as these children age, bipolar disorder surfaces regardless of whether they have received a diagnosis of ADHD or Asperger's syndrome. However, bipolar disorder is assumed to be a co-morbid (a not-so-parent-friendly term meaning "coexisting") possibility much more readily with Asperger's syndrome than with ADHD. Children diagnosed with Asperger's are more likely also to be evaluated and treated for bipolar disorder. Children diagnosed with ADHD, on the other hand, who exhibit anger, defiance, and resentfulness, generally receive a diagnosis of ODD. When we consider the implications of bipolar disorder remaining unidentified and untreated, we realize that many children are put at a tremendous risk for serious depressions and destructive rages. The consequences of bipolar disorder are of life-and-death significance.

Sadly, many young people with the ADHD/ODD diagnosis who really need an Asperger's/bipolar diagnosis never reach adulthood. Always feeling as if they're wrong, as if they're trouble, or as if they're not understood takes its toll upon their self-esteem. Without a proper diagnosis leading to professionals who understand and have compassion, these young adults become increasingly isolated from peers and others. Accordingly, this isolation sets them up for anger, paranoia, and depression. Genetically they are already programmed for such responses, so when their social environment encourages these emotions, these children will be at a greater risk of displaying them more acutely than the general population.

Most people equate bipolar disorder with mood swings. Certainly they are right; yet the general population cannot fathom how acute these changes in moods are. When most people think of mania, they think of someone who talks fast, doesn't sleep, and is generally on an emotional high. They are unaware that mania also compels people to serious paranoia, near-psychotic episodes, and actions that jeopardize their lives. For example, during one recent manic episode, a young lady believed that people were attempting to kill her. She refused to go to work, locked herself in her home, and armed herself with a gun. When her peers called to check on her, they realized she was acting abnormally. They contacted her family and physician, who recognized the danger in entering this young lady's home. They sent the police to disarm and hospitalize this woman. Once her bipolar disorder was treated, she returned to work and to a level of normalcy, recognizing that a near tragedy had been averted.

As dangerous as the paranoia becomes, the rages are also as fearful. Countless family members have suffered verbal and physical attacks or have watched in horror and disbelief as their homes have been ravaged by their children or spouses. The tension of walking on eggshells to avoid setting off a manic rage exhausts family members and creates a general atmosphere of fear in the home. Even after a manic episode passes and stability sets in, the family still has the physical and emotional reminders that these times are sure to come again.

After a time of stability, dark depressions set in. These depressions are so severe that the average person cannot comprehend their pain and immobility. One Asperger's syndrome patient describes the depression as "so painful that my skin hurts." Another sedates himself immediately after work because "getting through minute by minute is so painful and sleep is my escape."

During these depressive episodes, the pain becomes so unbearable that it is difficult to remember that it will pass. This is when suicide and even murder become the only alternative for relief. While in a serious depressive episode, one mother of young children plotted a combination murder-suicide. She planned to kill her children first and then herself. Fortunately, she turned to a friend before carrying out her plan. The friend took her to a doctor, who began immediate treatment.

Unfortunately, many young people who are seriously depressed do not reach out to others. These are the ones who, after years of being misunderstood and rejected, decide that suicide is better than continuing in depressive isolation. This was the case with one young man in his midtwenties who committed suicide despite having, by all appearances, a wonderful life. He was a successful diving coach, wealthy, and handsome. But his friends and associates noted that he was somewhat eccentric. According to his father, Greg had been diagnosed with ADHD—a diagnosis that his father contends "didn't offer any real answers to why he was so different." After Greg's death, his father ran across literature describing Asperger's syndrome. This syndrome, he believes, more adequately explained Greg's mood swings, attention difficulties, and isolation than did ADHD.

THE CHALLENGE AHEAD

Reminding myself of an important fact about autism, I began to consider the obstacles parents face when attempting to obtain an accurate diagnosis for their children. Because Asperger's syndrome is a developmental problem, its core deficit is a constant that looks very different at different developmental stages (I'll discuss this in greater detail in chapter 5). For instance, while Ben was diagnosed with ADHD as a first grader, in puberty he has become the poster child for Asperger's syndrome. He argues with authority, is aggressive, and has difficulties engaging in two-sided communication. Likewise, Sam received his diagnosis at age five; now, at age eleven he's exhibiting tendencies toward bipolar and depressive behaviors that commonly occur with Asperger's syndrome. As I consider the changes in my sons' symptoms, I've started to adopt a much wider view of the problem. With so many characteristics involved, it is no wonder that symptoms once thought to belong only to ADHD lead to other syndromes and more labels. And it is also no wonder that parents who aren't getting satisfactory diagnoses take their children to different doctors, who attach new labels but offer no new treatment options.

I am convinced that autism awareness must increase so physicians can better understand that many of the same characteristics defined as ADHD are also shared by autism. Also, while ADHD research still reaches symptom-based conclusions about diagnosis and treatment, autism research examines genetics and biomedical options for treatment. I'll explain this important distinction in chapter 4. Armed with this knowledge, physicians could glean greater treatment plans for their patients.

I recently encountered a quote that clarified my mission: "If you're only looking for ADHD you will never find autism."[3] With all the attention given to ADHD and its related symptoms, autism remains in the shadows. Yet I am certain that in the highest levels of research and the deepest degrees of parental struggles, ADHD and autism overlap.

For one mom trying to alter the paradigm of the number-one developmental disorder of our time, my battle has been of David-and-Goliath proportions. But I realize there is no greater calling in life than raising the children whom God has entrusted in our care. It is my prayer that this book provides support, help, and understanding to those also challenged by the blessings of God's most precious gifts, our children.

Chapter 2

Beginning with the Definitions

The Fine Lines Between Autistic Spectrum Disorders and Attention Deficit Disorders

Knowledge is the food of the soul.

PLATO

Obtaining accurate diagnoses for my sons was an important first step, but these diagnoses offered little clarity regarding the disorders themselves. As my time-consuming research into Asperger's and ADHD progressed, I ultimately discovered myself at a singular destination: the autistic spectrum. But in the beginning, the road there seemed impassable.

Interestingly, the information available to me from the autism camp offered a much more solid explanation of Sam's Asperger's syndrome and how to help him. Definitions and options for treatment of Ben's ADHD, however, made me feel trapped in a maze that offered no exit. The research and treatment options were full of dead ends and redundancies.

Because of my confusion, I decided to start where the physicians begin, with the DSM-IV-TR, the most current edition of the manual developed by the American Psychiatric Association to describe and classify mental disorders. Physicians use the DSM-IV-TR to diagnose their patients. It was here I discovered a classification of disorders known as pervasive development disorders (PDD). The syndromes listed under this catchall label are varied yet strikingly similar. In fact, they are so similar that the symptomatology of disorders such as Asperger's syndrome, PDD–NOS (pervasive developmental disorder–not otherwise specified), and even ADHD (which is *not* classified under the PDD heading) closely resemble one another—so much so that researchers and doctors have held to rigid criteria for diagnosing each disorder. The diagnostic criteria focus on three areas: behavior, communication, and socialization. To obtain a diagnosis, patients must exhibit deficits in all three areas. However, the severity of the deficit and the age of onset often determine the diagnosis. Consequently, instead of creating a method for a clear diagnosis, the criteria and labels used by professionals are confusing for patients and their caretakers.

When examining the criteria and ways in which autistic spectrum disorders are labeled in the medical community, the sources of the confusion become obvious. Autism is classified under PDD in the DSM-IV-TR. Along with autism are other disorders, such as Rett's Disorder, Childhood Disintegrative Disorder, Asperger's syndrome, and pervasive developmental disorder–not otherwise specified (PDD–NOS). Yet these disorders are so similar that Bernard Rimland, Ph.D., argues that the PDD label does more harm than good. He believes it offers no greater explanation of the developmental disorders commonly referred to as the autistic spectrum. He adds, "Quite apart from the misleading and inappropriate semantics of the term PDD is a very practical matter:

autistic children and adults unfortunate to have the PDD label affixed to them have often been—and continue to be—excluded from programs and services designated for those with autism, and which would benefit them."[1] In fact, Dr. Rimland concludes that "the PDD designation, along with its cumbersome bureaucratic language (i.e., PDD–NOS [pervasive developmental disorder–not otherwise specified] should be relegated to the Archives of Failed Attempts."[2] In other words, Dr. Rimland recognizes that the PDD and PDD–NOS labels are simply attempts by researchers to classify symptoms that are autistic in origin but do not fall neatly into any category. In other words, if a patient presents symptoms that are characteristic of autistic spectrum disorders, but all of the symptoms do not fit precisely into the categories established in the DSM-IV-TR, then the patient will most likely receive a diagnosis of PDD–NOS rather than autism. This is because physicians and psychologists are encouraged to view each disorder as distinct from the others. In this way, they can diagnose each disorder "differentially" (differently from the others). Patients are thereby labeled by their differential diagnosis.

According to the DSM-IV-TR, all of the disorders under the PDD heading "are characterized by severe and pervasive impairments in several areas of development: reciprocal social interaction skills, communication skills, or the presence of stereotyped behavior interests and activities. The qualitative impairments that define these conditions are distinctly deviant relevant to the individual's developmental level or mental age."[3] In other words, an accurate diagnosis often depends upon a person's age and the severity of the impairment *even though in some disorders the symptoms are strikingly similar.* This is especially true when discussing Asperger's syndrome and ADHD, even though ADHD is not categorized under PDD in the DSM-IV-TR. (While ADHD receives its own heading in the DSM-IV-TR, it is, however, classified as a developmental disorder.) To get a clear idea of how close these disorders are to one another, it is necessary to examine the symptoms and criteria associated with the diagnosis.

What Is Autism, and How Does It Relate to Asperger's Syndrome?

The Autism Society of America defines autism as a complex developmental disability that typically appears in the first three years of life. Autism is a result of a neurological disorder that affects the way the brain functions. In 1997 the Centers for Disease Control and Prevention estimated that autism and its associated behaviors occur in as many as one in five hundred people. Autism is four times more prevalent in boys than girls.[4]

What's often referred to as classical autism or "early infantile autism" is based upon the work of Leo Kanner, a Viennese physician. His famous paper "Autistic Disturbances of Affective Contact" was first published in 1943, while Kanner was working at Johns Hopkins. Kanner described children who exhibited a severe degree of social isolation, a lack of responsiveness to others, and serious language impairments. Often these children would experience delays in using language, exhibit echolalia or idiosyncratic expressions, and would seldom initiate conversation or interaction. These children also formed odd attachments to objects rather than people. Part of Kanner's evaluation included pricking these children lightly with a pin to test their responsiveness; yet they regularly would look at the pin rather than at the clinician, indicating an awareness of the object rather than of the person manipulating it. Likewise, these children were reported to form strong attachments to objects as areas of interest—especially trains, puzzles, stamps, and numbers—giving rise to our society's association of autism with the character portrayed by Dustin Hoffman in *Rain Man.*[5]

In 1944 Hans Asperger, a pediatrician also from Vienna, published "Autistic Psychopathy in Childhood," a paper that documented his observations of children with social and communicative impairments who also exhibited a diverse range of cognitive skills and abilities. Unlike Kanner's subjects, Asperger's patients showed little developmental delay in language acquisition. In fact, some had exceptional vocabularies, though their comprehension of language was not as sophisticated as it initially appeared. For example, in terms of sentence structures and vocabulary, Asperger's subjects were more functional in discourse. Asperger's patients also exhibited strong attachments to objects and areas of interest and would often direct their conversations to these areas despite the effect upon their listener. In this way Asperger's patients, too, exhibited a degree of unawareness of others, focusing instead on an interest instead of a person, much like Kanner's subjects would focus upon the pin.[6]

According to Maria Asperger Felder, M.D., in her foreword to *Asperger Syndrome,* from 1949 on "Hans Asperger published several articles comparing the disorder he had been describing with the one that Leo Kanner had called 'early infantile autism'. He pointed out...the characteristics that both disorders had in common (impairment in social responsiveness or interest in others, and serious communicative impairment)."[7] Nevertheless, the main difference between Kanner's subjects and Asperger's was the effect of intelligence on the impairments. Asperger believed that the fundamental deficits of autism were just as severe. Yet he did not ignore the effect of IQ on his subjects. In fact, according to Uta Frith in her book *Autism and Asperger Syndrome,* "It is possible for the Asperger person to learn social routines so well that he or she may strike others as merely eccentric.... Of course, such hard won adaptation is achieved only at a price. The Asperger person will have had to learn with great effort what others learn quite naturally."[8]

Lorna Wing, M.D., in her book *The Autistic Spectrum,* suggests that despite the similarities between Kanner's and Asperger's subjects, each scientist considered the onset of the developmental delays to occur at different stages: Asperger noted onset to be after three years or when children entered school, whereas Kanner originally thought onset to be between birth and thirty months.[9] Building upon these criteria for differentiating autism from Asperger's syndrome, the DSM-IV-TR maintains that Asperger's syndrome can be distinguished from autism by the lack of delay or deviance in early language development. However, it is only recently that Asperger's syndrome has been accepted as a subtype of autism belonging on the autistic spectrum.

Until 1981 the scientific community held to a rigid and limited view of autism that relied upon Kanner's timetable for language delay as well as impaired cognitive or mental abilities. When Dr. Wing used the term "Asperger's syndrome" to describe a group of patients whose pathologies were very similar to the personalities and abilities described by Asperger, she sparked a debate about degrees of severity along the autistic spectrum and whether Asperger's syndrome is a form of autism. In the group Dr. Wing described, some of the patients demonstrated language impairments and social aloofness when very young, but then they went on to develop normal speech patterns and a need to socialize. In this sense they developed beyond the traditional diagnosis of autism. They still demonstrated significant difficulties in social skills and reciprocal dialogue as well as very narrow areas of intense interest, characteristics that closely resembled Asperger's original group of children.

Over time, the scientific community has come to recognize that Asperger's syndrome is indeed a milder form of autism and belongs on the autistic spectrum.[10]

The DSM-IV-TR states, "Asperger's Disorder is characterized by stereotyped behaviors and interests and by more severely impaired social interaction."[11] Some examples of stereotyped behaviors are probably familiar to you: rocking, head nodding, hand flapping, finger movements, thumb sucking—all of these behaviors are ones we see in our children from time to time. Yet to obtain a professional diagnosis of Asperger's syndrome, a person must meet the following criteria as taken from the DSM-IV-TR:

A. Qualitative impairment in social interaction, as manifested by at least two of the following:
   - Marked impairment in the use of multiple nonverbal behaviors such as eye-to-eye gaze, facial expression, body postures, and gestures to regulate social interaction
   - Failure to develop peer relationships appropriate to developmental level
   - A lack of spontaneous seeking to share enjoyment, interests, or achievements with other people (e.g., by a lack of showing, bringing, or pointing out objects of interest to other people)
   - Lack of social or emotional reciprocity

B. Restricted repetitive and stereotyped patterns of behavior, interests, and activities, as manifested by at least one of the following:
   - Encompassing preoccupation with one or more stereotyped and restricted patterns of interest that is abnormal either in intensity or focus

- Apparently inflexible adherence to specific, nonfunctional routines or rituals
- Stereotyped and repetitive motor mannerisms (e.g., hand or finger flapping or twisting, or complex whole-body movements)
- Persistent preoccupation with parts of objects

C. The disturbance causes clinically significant impairment in social, occupational, or other important areas of functioning.

D. There is no clinically significant general delay in language (e.g., single words used by age 2 years, communicative phrases used by age 3 years).

E. There is no clinically significant delay in cognitive development or in the development of age-appropriate self-help skills, adaptive behavior (other than in social interaction), and curiosity about the environment in childhood.

F. Criteria are not met for another specific Pervasive Development Disorder or Schizophrenia.[12]

According to Dr. Wing, a diagnosis of Asperger's disorder often comes after a child starts school, especially if there has been no significant delay in language.[13] This is because in the school setting, the impairments in social interaction along with the inability to engage in reciprocal conversation emerge most readily.[14] In other words, a child's inability to take turns in conversation, read another's body language, and understand the unspoken rules for behavior and play appear quite readily in a classroom environment. Likewise, it is during this period that the rigidity or insistence upon sameness of children with Asperger's syndrome becomes apparent.[15] Consequently, these children do not adapt well to new routines or changes in established patterns. Thus even shifting from task to task during the course of a day can be upsetting to a child with Asperger's syndrome.

If you're familiar with ADHD, perhaps you're beginning to see that it has a lot in common with Asperger's syndrome. Both are typically diagnosed in school-age children, and they both affect how a child relates socially to others. I'll discuss these similarities in more detail in the next chapter. However, to understand more fully how ADHD is currently diagnosed, we must return to the DSM-IV-TR guidelines.

WHAT IS ADHD?

By far the most popular developmental disorder is ADHD. The DSM-IV-TR estimates that ADHD affects 3 to 7 percent of all school-age children with a 4:1 ratio of diagnosis for boys to girls.[16] In fact, you may be reading this book right now because your child was diagnosed with ADHD. Like Asperger's syndrome, ADHD is a developmental disorder that becomes most evident after a child begins school. It is in this setting that inattention and/or impulsivity often cause disruptions severe enough to warrant medical attention. According to the DSM-IV-TR, the central "feature of Attention Deficit/Hyperactivity Disorder is a persistent pattern of inattention and/or hyperactivity/impulsivity that is more frequently displayed and more severe than is typically observed in individuals at a comparable level of development."[17] Usually the initial diagnosis occurs around age seven.

The diagnostic criteria for ADHD occur in the DSM-IV-TR as follows:

A. Either (1) or (2):

(1) Six (or more) of the following symptoms of *inattention* have persisted for at least 6 months to a degree that is maladaptive and inconsistent with developmental level:

(a) Often fails to give close attention to details or makes careless mistakes in schoolwork, work, or other activities

(b) Often has difficulty sustaining attention in tasks or play activities

(c) Often does not seem to listen when spoken to directly

(d) Often does not follow through on instructions and fails to finish schoolwork, chores, or duties in the workplace (not due to oppositional behavior or failure to understand instructions)

(e) Often has difficulty organizing tasks and activities

(f) Often avoids, dislikes, or is reluctant to engage in tasks that require sustained mental effort (such as schoolwork or homework)

(g) Often loses things necessary for tasks or activities (e.g., toys, school assignments, pencils, books, or tools)

(h) is often easily distracted by extraneous stimuli

(i) is often forgetful in daily activities

(2) Six (or more) of the following symptoms of *hyperactivity-impulsivity* have persisted for at least 6 months to a degree that is maladaptive and inconsistent with developmental level:

Hyperactivity

(a) often fidgets with hands or feet or squirms in seat

(b) often leaves seat in classroom or in other situations in which remaining in seat is expected

(c) often runs about or climbs excessively in situations in which it is inappropriate (in adolescents or adults, may be limited to subjective feelings of restlessness)
(d) often has difficulty playing or engaging in leisure activities quietly
(e) is often "on the go" or often acts as if "driven by a motor"
(f) often talks excessively

Impulsivity

(g) often blurts out answers before questions have been completed
(h) often has difficulty awaiting turn
(i) often interrupts or intrudes on others (e.g., butts into conversations or games)

B. Some hyperactive-impulsive or inattentive symptoms that caused impairment were present before age 7 years.

C. Some impairment from the symptoms is present in two or more settings (e.g., at school or work and at home).

D. There must be clear evidence of clinically significant impairment in social, academic, or occupational functioning.

E. The symptoms do not occur exclusively during the course of a Pervasive Developmental Disorder, Schizophrenia, or other Psychotic Disorder and are not better accounted for by another mental disorder (e.g., Mood Disorder, Anxiety Disorder, Dissociative Disorder, or a Personality Disorder).[18]

To attempt to account for the varying degrees of impairment, researchers have developed subtypes of ADHD and base their diagnoses upon combinations of the above diagnostic criteria.

- *Attention-Deficit/Hyperactivity Disorder, Combined Type:* If both criteria A1 and A2 are met for the past six months.
- *Attention-Deficit/Hyperactivity Disorder, Predominantly Inattentive Type:* If criterion A1 is met but criterion A2 is not met for the past six months.
- *Attention-Deficit/Hyperactivity Disorder, Predominantly Hyperactive-Impulsive Type:* If criterion A2 is met but criterion A1 is not met for the past six months.
- In addition to all of these subtypes, ADHD also has a catchall category: *Attention-Deficit/Hyperactivity Disorder–Not Otherwise Specified.* Like the catchall category PDD–NOS under the PDD classification, this category is for patients who exhibit the symptoms of inattention or hyperactivity/impulsivity but who do not completely meet the criteria for ADHD.[19]

One important point must be made concerning the ADHD criterion E: It is here where the differential diagnosis between ADHD and autism is usually made. While autism recognizes ADHD as a disorder that coexists or is co-morbid with autistic spectrum disorders, the reverse is not true: ADHD does *not* recognize the co-morbidity of these disorders. Consequently, when a patient receives a diagnosis of ADHD, the buck stops there, so to speak. In other words, if a child presents enough symptoms to qualify for an ADHD diagnosis, physicians usually look no further to see if other disorders may be underlying the ADHD symptoms. Thus the child is treated for ADHD only.

However, when physicians who are trained in autism screen for autistic spectrum disorders, a different problem arises. Oftentimes, depending upon the stage of a child's development, the symptoms of autism or Asperger's syndrome are not severe enough to meet the stringent criteria used for diagnosis. Consequently, parents are told to take the child to an ADHD specialist for treatment. What often occurs, as it did in Sam's case, is that the specialists in ADHD treat these children as extreme cases, giving them labels of ODD and even Conduct Disorder (CD) while offering little hope in terms of true understanding or help. However, as Uta Frith points out in her translation of Asperger's work, "It can't be presumed that all the essential features and only the essential features will at once be identified."[20] Once again we see that time and development will affect diagnosis.

Diagnosis is a complex matter, and the brief information I've offered here is merely to help point out the fine lines that separate our existing definitions of the disorders. Chapter 4 is devoted to a more thorough discussion of diagnosis itself.

THE AUTISTIC STIGMA

As I searched for explanations and answers to help my sons, I realized that there was a huge discrepancy between autism awareness and awareness of ADHD. The limited knowledge that we have about autistic spectrum disorders, including a milder form of autism such as Asperger's syndrome, reflects a fundamental fear of autism in our society. By nature we fear those who are different from us—especially when they behave in ways that are unusual and respond to the world differently than others. Thus most people fear those labeled as autistic. This fear is most likely tied to the predominant view of autism based upon the portrait of the severely autistic man in *Rain Man.* What mother in her right mind would want to obtain a diagnosis of autism for her child—particularly when autism is so closely tied to the image of the silent withdrawn youngster or the adult idiot savant? Likewise, what physician would want to levy a life sentence of autism against a child? No, a diagnosis of ADHD is much more palatable and acceptable than one of Asperger's syndrome, since an ADHD diagnosis seems to offer a much brighter future than a child with autism. Similarly, a label of ADHD also defies the stigma that the autism label oftentimes presents. And with so many subtypes available, obtaining a diagnosis under one of ADHD's categories is much easier, not to mention more common or trendy, than a diagnosis of Asperger's syndrome or autism.

However, the person with Asperger's syndrome is most often very gifted and blessed with an extraordinarily creative mind. Dr. Wing's works gave me great comfort about Sam's diagnosis and offered me so much hope for his future. Through additional research I discovered that some of our greatest inventors allegedly had Asperger's syndrome, including Thomas Jefferson, Albert Einstein, and more recently, Bill Gates, who reportedly displays such autistic tendencies as rocking, not making eye contact, and "not having the social skills necessary to enter a group conversation."[21] Clearly, our society views Gates as an eccentric man, but we also recognize that he possesses a unique genius that has benefited us all.

A central theme I have noticed in all the descriptions of Asperger and his observations is that he was fascinated by this group of individuals that he studied. Even though he acknowledged their difficulties with communication and socialization, and he confirmed how challenging these children are to raise, he also recognized their ability to be exceptional—a view I share with great passion: "In some cases, however, the problems are compensated by a high level of original thought and experience. This can often lead to exceptional achievements in later life."[22] Sam's current teacher has expressed a similar view. While exhausted by his social handicaps and his extreme behaviors, she is in awe of his unique ability to think in a creative and original way despite his struggles. And while her view of these individuals is indeed a blessing, she is the exception rather than the rule. Nevertheless, I believe more people would share her view if only they understood these precious individuals and Asperger's syndrome more fully.

Chapter 3

Which Is It: Autism or ADHD?

The Similarities Are Not Coincidental

Let the wise listen and add to their learning,
and let the discerning get guidance.
PROVERBS 1:5

What is a mother to do when confronted with two disorders that present themselves so similarly in terms of symptoms yet are considered unique by the scientific community? More research, of course. After serving as president of the Metro Louisville Chapter of CHADD, as well as assisting the Kentucky State Advisory Council of CHADD, I realized that my children's needs were not being addressed through ADHD research. In fact, it was while serving on the state advisory council that my friend Joni suggested I look at current autism research to understand the severity of my son Sam's ADHD.

Like most parents, I immediately rejected the notion that my son could have autism. After all, he was the opposite of Kanner's silent and aloof poster child. My Sam was "in your face," verbally advanced, active, defiant, impulsive, and hyperactive—not at all withdrawn or quiet. *How could he possibly have an autistic spectrum disorder?* I wondered. However, after my initial defensiveness dissipated, I became willing to see what the autism researchers offered as answers.

I quickly discovered that while ADHD research focused on the features of the disorder, autism research examined the disorder for root causes from which to develop treatments. Despite the difference in the way each camp approaches its disorder, both autistic spectrum disorders and ADHD are developmental disorders that share similar features and affect children in three central areas: communication, social interaction, and behavior.

This is where the confusion between these disorders arises. Couldn't what researchers and parents often see as distinct symptoms at particular stages of development be a continuum of the same disorder as it manifests itself at different times? If so, then it is the combination of the symptoms themselves along with the severity of the symptoms that most likely determines whether a child is diagnosed with an autistic spectrum disorder or with ADHD. Of course, a proper diagnosis based upon this combination would hinge upon there being enough awareness of autistic spectrum disorders and the similarities they share with ADHD to obtain an accurate assessment.

As of now, however, our medical and educational professionals are not trained to recognize the similarities between these disorders. In fact, these professionals are directed by the American Pediatric Association to screen for ADHD, but autistic spectrum disorders are not even addressed. According to the latest clinical practice guideline presented concurrently in *Pediatric 2000* and at the conference Advancing Children's Health 2000, developed for pediatricians and primary care physicians, "the first recommendation is that when a child aged 6-12 years presents with inattention, hyperactivity, impulsivity, academic underachievement, or behavioral problems, primary care physicians should initiate an evaluation for ADHD."[1] Thus pediatricians and educators often are not aware that autistic spectrum disorders may be a diagnostic option, giving rise to a blindness that denies proper diagnosis and treatment and thwarts parents' search for information to help them understand their children.

Likewise, even though autism researchers acknowledge the comorbidity of autistic spectrum disorders and ADHD, they still approach each disorder as distinctly different. This separateness is revealed in *The Handbook of Autism and Pervasive Developmental Disorders:* "As in children without autism, attention deficits and hyperactivity in children with autism may present differently at different ages or levels of development."[2] The phrase "as in children without autism" illustrates the fundamental acceptance of autism and ADHD as distinctly different disorders. However, when examining the similarities in terms of origins of deficits, communication, social competency, and behavior, the distinction between these disorders blurs, leaving one to question whether ADHD, too, belongs on the autistic spectrum.

SIMILARITIES IN POPULATIONS AND SCREENING TOOLS

Numerous similarities exist between the ways autistic spectrum disorders and ADHD are presented in the available literature. One of the most common is the way each group of researchers identifies the population most affected by the disorder. For example, according to the National Information Center for Children and Youth with Disabilities Fact Sheet on Autism and Pervasive Developmental Disorders, the incidence of autism and PDD is "four times more common in boys than girls,"[3] a statistic that clearly links this disorder primarily to males. Likewise, a recent report of the Surgeon General states that "boys are four times more likely to have [ADHD] than girls,"[4] and autism researcher Dr. B. J. Freeman, a professor at the UCLA School of Medicine and Neuropsychiatric Institute states, "Boys are affected more often than girls by a ratio of 4:1."[5] Thus it is easy to see the commonality in populations affected by these disorders.

The ways in which patients are screened for autism and ADHD are shockingly alike in content. Each side uses a checklist of behaviors and social characteristics to help parents, medical professionals, and educators evaluate a child. Interestingly, the characteristics and features highlighted by each checklist are identical to one another (see Table 3.1).

What is evident from Table 3.1 is that the disorders themselves are nearly identical. The major difference is primarily *in the degree of severity.* When examining the major characteristics of each disorder side-by-side and seeing that they are so closely related, the similarities become quite evident—but only after a person has been trained to see them. I once conducted an in-service training for teachers and presented them with the autism checklist, but I didn't label it. All of them recognized what they believed to be the major characteristics of ADHD. Consequently, because of their bias toward ADHD and their lack of awareness about the characteristics of autistic spectrum disorders, they were shocked to learn it was a checklist for autism. However, all were eager to learn more about the relationship between these disorders so they could better help parents and students.

Table 3.1 Checklists for Behaviors in ADHD and Autism

AUTISM CHECKLIST[6]	ADHD CHECKLIST[7]
Difficulty mixing with other children	Cannot talk or play quietly; disrupts others with talk or actions; difficulty awaiting turn in games or activities
No real fear of dangers	Engages in potentially dangerous activities. Plays without normal caution or consideration of consequences
Tantrums: Displays extreme distress for no apparent reason Inappropriate giggling or laughing	Severe temper tantrums Interrupts, disrupts, talks and acts inappropriately
May not want cuddling or act cuddly	When younger, difficulty accepting soothing or holding
Noticeable physical overactivity or extreme underactivity	Always on the move, overactive, even during sleep
Little or no eye contact	Often does not seem to listen when spoken to directly
Works impulsively; often makes careless mistakes; work is sloppy	Often does not give close attention to details or makes careless mistakes in schoolwork or other activities
Uneven gross/fine motor skills	Uneven gross/fine motor skills

I KNOW I'M CLUMSY: SIMILARITIES IN MOTOR-SKILL IMPAIRMENT

One major area highlighted by both camps is motor skills. Both autistic spectrum disorders and ADHD discuss uneven gross and fine motor skills when describing their populations. For instance, the American Academy of Neurology and the Child Neurology Society recently published their diagnostic guidelines for front-line physicians in autism. In these guidelines, they state that "impairments of gross and fine motor function are reported as being common in autistic individuals."[8] Accordingly, in his book *Asperger's Syndrome: A Guide for Parents and Professionals,* Tony Attwood describes the following motor function problems that are typical for Asperger's syndrome children:

- ungainly movements in walking and running
- problems with timing and accuracy in ball throwing and catching
- difficulties with balance such as balancing on one foot with eyes shut or walking a straight line
- poor handwriting
- impulsive, hasty approaches to fine motor tasks resulting in mistakes
- difficulty in keeping rhythm[9]

In fact, clumsiness and awkwardness are so prevalent in children with Asperger's syndrome that autism researcher Christopher Gillberg argues that the DSM should be revised to include clumsiness as a diagnostic criterion.[10]

The DSM-IV-TR guidelines for ADHD also address the areas of gross and fine motor skills when discussing characteristics of ADHD. One of the criterion, criterion D, in the DSM-IV-TR for ADHD says "there must be clear evidence of clinically significant impairment in social, academic, or occupational functioning."[11] Along these same lines, the DSM-IV-TR also states that with ADHD, children's "work is often messy and performed carelessly,"[12] indicating an impulsive, hasty approach as noted in autistic research. Accordingly, recent papers presented at the CHADD Conferences (1998 and 2000) discuss the following symptoms to look for in children with ADHD:

- impaired coordination
- poor or illegible handwriting
- poor eye-hand coordination in sports
- soft neurological signs, e.g., *clumsy* (emphasis added)
- problems with bimanual coordination
- difficulties balancing on one foot[13]

It is evident from these two lists of motor problems found in both autism and ADHD that virtually the same functions are impaired in both groups.

DON'T TOUCH ME! SIMILARITIES IN ERRATIC SENSORY RESPONSES

Another area that nearly everyone familiar with autism cites as a characteristic of the disorder is erratic sensory responses. Children with autistic spectrum disorders process tactile, visual, and auditory stimuli differently from other children. According to a recent article, "42 to 88 percent of individuals with autism have sensory processing abilities that are aberrant and include responses like over- or underresponding to environmental stimuli or having unpredictable responses to sensory stimuli."[14]

One Asperger's syndrome patient describes being very sensitive to things she touches and that touch her: "No perfumes, hand lotions, creams, Chapstick, suntan lotion.... I'm fairly sensitive to temperatures too, I hate being cold most of all."[15] Other writers describe sensory issues centered on food textures and appearance.[16] Similarly, my son Sam, who was diagnosed with Asperger's syndrome, would scream while in the shower because the sensation of the water against his skin was excruciating. Dr. Temple Grandin describes her struggles with tactile sensory responses in her article "My Experiences with Visual Thinking Sensory Problems and Communication Difficulties." Here Dr. Grandin describes her responses to tactile stimulation from being held or from the feeling of a change of clothing: "I pulled away when people tried to hug me, because being touched sent an overwhelming tidal wave of stimulation through my body. I wanted to feel the comforting feeling of being held, but...the effect on my nervous system was overwhelming. It was an approach-avoid situation but sensory overstimulation caused the avoidance, not anger or fear."[17] Thus sensory stimulation that seems normal to most people can cause pain, confusion, and even detachment in people with autistic spectrum disorders.

Sensory stimulation and avoidance are not limited to autism. My son Ben, who was diagnosed with ADHD, screamed whenever I washed his hair because of the pain he felt. He also reacted strongly to itching caused by tags in his clothing. He regularly would rip holes in the necklines of his shirts in an effort to remove the source of extreme discomfort. Dr. Grandin notes that "small itches and scratches that most people ignored were torture"[18]—a response I saw embodied in Ben's reactions to his clothing.

Current research indicates that the responses to sensory stimuli found in children with autistic spectrum disorders are present in children with ADHD. For instance, an article for CBS *HealthWatch* echoes Dr. Grandin's assessment of a child's reaction to the sensation of being held: "One of the most painful events a parent may experience is an abrupt and aggressive attack that may occur after cuddling a young ADHD child. Often this reaction seems to be caused *not by anger but by overstimulation*"[19] (emphasis added). In this article, then, you can see ADHD researchers using the same language and reasoning to explain identical responses to identical situations found in both autism and ADHD. Likewise, hypersensitivity to touch, sights, sounds, and other stimuli that would seem minor to others is noted in this article, though the author does not reach any conclusions about its significance.[20]

Not only do tactile and visual stimuli affect the autistic person, so do environment and noise. Erin, daughter of my writing partner, Becky, would shriek in pain while riding with the car windows rolled down because the sound of the wind in her ears caused extreme discomfort. Similarly, Dr. Grandin also documented her struggles with everyday activities like going to shopping centers or talking on phones in noisy areas because of her sound sensitivity: "My hearing is like having a sound amplifier set on maximum loudness. My ears are like a microphone that picks up and amplifies sound. I have two choices: (1) turn my ears on and get deluged with sound or (2) shut my ears off."[21] However, to shut out the stimuli one must resort to "tuning out," another way of describing inattentiveness.

This same tendency is noted in ADHD literature with regard to distractibility. According to *What Is Attention Deficit Disorder?* the concept of inattention with regard to ADHD may be misleading. Instead of inattention, these writers assert that "because ADHD children are usually distracted by over-stimulating situations, some learn to compensate by developing a kind of 'super concentration' " and as a result become overattentive or so absorbed in a project as to become unable to shift attention.[22] It is this same tendency that is described in autism literature time and again; however, now it is being recognized in ADHD as well.

BIRDS OF A FEATHER FLOCK TOGETHER: SIMILARITIES IN CO-MORBID DISORDERS

Another diagnostic similarity these disorders share is that of co-morbidity, or coexisting conditions and syndromes. Both autistic spectrum disorders and ADHD often present other disorders, such as:

- language and communication disorders
- sleep disorders
- reading problems
- bipolar disorder
- mood and anxiety disorders
- depression
- learning disorders
- oppositional defiant disorders
- obsessive compulsive disorders

Drs. Church, Alisanski, and Amanullah found that of the middle-school-age children in their study "38% had a secondary diagnosis of a behaviour disorder (oppositional defiant disorder, conduct disorder)."[23] Along this same line, a recent article in the *Clinical Psychiatry News* states that in one study of nine hundred Asperger's syndrome patients, 65 percent had attention deficit hyperactivity disorder.[24] Likewise, Drs. Ami Klin and Fred Volkmar found that one of Asperger's syndrome's frequently co-morbid conditions included ADHD, as well as ODD, and personality disorders such as depression[25] (though we must note here that most autism researchers do not differentiate between the behaviors associated with autistic spectrum disorders and ODD). The

DSM-IV-TR also states that "symptoms of overactivity and inattention are frequent in Asperger's Disorder, and indeed many individuals with this condition receive a diagnosis of ADHD prior to the diagnosis of AD [Asperger disorder]."[26] Asperger himself noted that such children have a tremendous number of attention deficits. Significantly, the DSM-IV-TR also recognizes that Asperger's syndrome is associated with "a number of other mental disorders, including Depressive Disorders" under which bipolar is listed.[27] Bipolar disorder occurs with both autism and ADHD.

Like researchers in autism, researchers in ADHD also recognize the existence of co-morbid disorders. The American Academy of Pediatrics, under recommendation five for primary care physicians, states that "evaluation of the child with ADHD should include assessment for coexisting conditions"[28] such as the ones listed on the previous page.

At a recent annual meeting of the American Academy of Pediatrics, Mark Wolraich, M.D., presented a paper in which he detailed some of the more common co-morbid disorders occurring with ADHD. He states that co-morbid conditions of ADHD include oppositional-defiant or conduct disorder, language and communication disorders, and personality disorders in adolescence. Specifically, according to Dr. Wolraich, 30 to 50 percent of children diagnosed with ADHD have language disorders (including problems with pragmatic language), and 30 to 65 percent have oppositional-defiant and conduct disorders.[29] Additionally, with regard to mood disorders, an estimated 25 percent of children with ADHD become bipolar adults, while nearly 70 percent of ADHD people may suffer from depressive episodes.[30]

As you can see, Asperger's syndrome and ADHD share nearly identical patterns of co-morbidity, further suggesting that these disorders are indeed related. Unfortunately, because the DSM-IV-TR separates autism and ADHD and because ADHD researchers assume that autism and ADHD are unrelated, they do not recognize that the disorders they see as co-morbid are highly indicative of autistic spectrum disorders—especially milder forms of autistic disorders like Asperger's syndrome.

LIKE-MINDEDNESS: SIMILARITIES IN THE EXECUTIVE FUNCTION AND CORE DEFICITS

In their independent searches for the causes of autistic spectrum disorders and ADHD, researchers have examined the brain for core deficits. While both sides target various structures of the brain for different deficits, the area that appears to be responsible both for responses to people and environment is the executive function. Researchers in both autism and ADHD locate the seat of the executive function in the frontal lobe areas of the brain.[31]

According to recent autism research, executive function allows the normal person to shift attention flexibly, inhibit irrelevant responses, create goal-directed behavior, and solve problems in a planned, strategic way.[32] In other words, the executive function permits a person to act deliberately within an environment by shifting attention easily, by regulating impulsive responses, by setting and seeking to achieve goals, and by using reasoning, foresight, and premeditation to solve problems. Thus it is this function of the brain that controls attentiveness, inhibits behavior, and allows a person to act purposefully upon the surrounding social environment. Consequently, when there is a deficit in executive function, it manifests itself through inattentiveness, distractibility, and impulsivity—three areas acknowledged in both the autism and ADHD checklists for behaviors presented in Table 3.1.

Researchers in ADHD also point to deficits in the executive function as potential causes of the disorder. Dr. Russell Barkley, a leading researcher in ADHD, recently published his model of the executive function and the deficits associated with ADHD. In his search for the origins and explanations of ADHD, Dr. Barkley constructed a hybrid model of the executive function based upon the most current neuropsychological research in ADHD. His model implicates the identical regions that autism researchers associate with the executive function (the frontal lobe) and the same processes (working memory, behavioral inhibition, motor control, verbal communication, and organizational abilities).[33]

Consequently, both ADHD and autism research bears out a common set of behaviors and processes linked with impairments in the executive function of the brain. Some of the most obvious and familiar to mothers with children diagnosed with ADHD or Asperger's syndrome are the following:

- the inability to keep a number of items in working memory, such as multiple directions or tasks
- poor temporal judgment
- weak organization skills
- the inability to plan and prioritize
- the inability to assign attention to competing stimuli
- subtle language/communication problems
- problems in operating within social environments

Children who exhibit more severe cases of ADHD often share many of the characteristics and features with children at the high-functioning end of the autistic spectrum—particularly in the all-too-familiar areas of communication, social integration, and behavior.

WHAT DO YOU MEAN I DON'T UNDERSTAND? SIMILARITIES IN COMMUNICATION DISORDERS

The ability to express oneself and to understand another is fundamental to all human interaction. Even Scripture recognizes the role that communication plays in relationships: "Undoubtedly there are all sorts of languages in the world, yet none of them is without meaning. If then I do not grasp the meaning of what someone is saying, I am a foreigner to the speaker, and he is a foreigner to me" (1 Corinthians 14:10-11). Effective communication presupposes that the speaker is able to express himself verbally through language as well as interpret nonverbal messages from others. Unfortunately, impairments in communication are markers for both autistic spectrum disorders and ADHD. However, as with the other similarities discussed thus far, the major difference lies not in the nature of the impairments but rather in the severity of them.

Autism researchers and speech pathologists have recognized for some time that verbal or language abilities can be misleading when trying to diagnose autism, especially Asperger's syndrome. One point of confusion with diagnosing Asperger's in very young children is that their language development appears normal—that is, there are no significant delays in language or speech. However, once these children enter school, language again can be deceptive. The difficulty, according to speech-language pathologist Diane Twachtman-Cullen, is that children who have Asperger's "possess a language system that is at least functional, if not downright impressive, at least from the perspective of vocabulary (i.e., content) and grammar/syntax (i.e., form)."[34] In other words, many Asperger's syndrome children possess a large vocabulary and have a good grasp of the normal syntactical patterns of speech—a characteristic that most people would consider a strength but which is, for children with Asperger's, a serious liability. This is because it often masks their problems mastering other life skills. The DSM-IV-TR bears this out in its section on Asperger's syndrome: "Good verbal abilities may, to some extent, mask the severity of the child's social dysfunction and may also mislead caregivers and teachers—that is, caregivers and teachers may focus on a child's good verbal skills but be insufficiently aware of the problems in other areas."[35]

Yet regardless of how proficient Asperger's syndrome children are in language skills, they have great difficulty with the literal interpretation of language. For example, Dr. Lorna Wing cites the case in which a small boy was told to dry a teapot on the outside. He obediently took it outdoors "to wipe it dry."[36] Similarly, I once overheard Sam telling a friend that a birth control pill is "something people take to keep them calm during birth." Likewise, as Becky and Erin passed a sign for a new housing development that read "Only three lots left," Erin commented, "Oh, the rest must have stayed." As you can see, although it can lead to humorous situations, the inability to understand language beyond a literal level indicates a serious lack of comprehension.

These children are able to use language but are unable to comprehend the multiple levels of meaning associated with it, which seriously affects social interactions and, consequently, all aspects of life. For instance, according to Dr. Lisa Blakemore-Brown, in cases where a child has solid verbal skills but an underlying problem with comprehending prosody, the misinterpretations can lead to rages and negative reactions from others.[37] A good example of this occurs with Becky's daughter, Erin. She often confuses compliments for sarcasm, which sets off terrible arguments leading to hurt feelings and mistrust. Likewise, my son Sam will commonly confuse a directive such as "Put your shoes on the porch" as a hard fast rule. Consequently, he puts his shoes on the porch every time rather than only in response to that one-time instruction.

Dr. Wing also notes another characteristic of language that affects social interactions is the "tendency to talk on...or to ask repetitive questions regardless of the answers, or most irritating of all, to engage in arguments that are endless because the child always finds a new objection to whatever is suggested."[38] This characteristic is very similar to the excessive talking and impulsivity in speech ascribed to ADHD.

Verbal abilities also mislead teachers and parents of ADHD children. However, often in the case of ADHD, the focus is upon the excessive use of verbal abilities to the point of disruption. The DSM-IV-TR addresses this aspect of language use under the concepts of hyperactivity, as well as impulsivity (which we have already seen is linked to a deficit in executive function), and lists these symptoms: often talks excessively; often blurts out answers before questions have been completed; often interrupts or intrudes on others.[39] Not surprisingly, an ADHD child's command and use of language is often tied to impaired inhibition; or, as Dr. Russell Barkley contends, impulsivity and hyperactivity are evidence of a central impairment in the behavioral inhibition system, thereby suggesting a neuropathology that underlies the ADHD child's approach to language.[40] This neuropathology implies that, at some level, the ADHD child is unable to regulate the impulsive nature of his speech; however, because the impulsivity is also tied to behavior, this creates a situation where a child's use of language is seen as willful and subject to self-control.[41]

Drs. Edward Hallowell and John Ratey confirm this idea in their book *Driven to Distraction:* "Researchers and clinicians have framed ADD as an inability to stop receiving messages rather than as an inability to receive the right messages." They continue by asserting that the

ADD individual is unable to filter stimuli from the environment, describing this individual as "captive to the events of the external world." What emerges from their view is a portrait of someone who focuses or attends to everything rather than suffering from the inability to concentrate at all.[42] This model ascribes mistaken language, social and behavioral cues to the hurried nature of the ADHD mind—a mind in which time collapses (or as autism would say with regard to executive function—a mind with poor temporal judgement). In this mind, "instead of being able to carve out discrete activities that would create a sensation of separate moments, the person cannot stop the relentless flow of events." Continuing with this reasoning then, Drs. Hallowell and Ratey contend that the "failure to form intimate relationships is the inability to pause long enough even to listen to the other person, let alone to understand and respect the other's needs." Consequently, they assert that "the impulsivity, the lack of planning and the outbursts are the inability to restrain the flow of action and feeling."[43]

Autistic theory, on the other hand, suggests that the central underlying problem in communication is the inability to comprehend the nonverbal aspects of social discourse. These aspects, also known as pragmatics, account for two-way interaction through tendencies like eye contact, taking turns in conversation, body language and signals, interpretation of facial expressions, the ability to modulate tone and volume according to context. Speech pathologist Diane Twachtman-Cullen states that anywhere between 90 to 93 percent of meaning is carried by these nonverbal aspects of communication.[44] Asperger's syndrome patients, however, cannot comprehend the subtle meanings expressed through intonation and other features that carry meaning. For example, in these children "the appreciation of paralinguistic cues [inflection, stress, tone, and facial expression] and an understanding of their essential role in communication often go unnoticed"[45]; consequently, people with Asperger's syndrome must attend so carefully to the various aspects of "communicative and language behavior," they are likely to miss the central cues that carry the speaker's meaning. Therefore, they fail to comprehend the finer aspects of communication and meaning even though they often possess superior verbal skills. Thus the core deficit in Asperger's syndrome is a deficit of comprehension that leads to mistaken language, social, and behavioral cues.

Interestingly, the impulsivity and inattention that ADHD researchers claim as core deficits may in fact stem from a more basic deficit in the executive function—a deficit that affects comprehension of both verbal and, more important, nonverbal communication and social cues.

WHY CAN'T I PLAY YOUR WAY? SIMILARITIES IN SOCIAL DEFICITS

Unfortunately, according to Dr. Paul Elliott, the ADHD field maintains the prevailing belief that a diagnosis can be made upon the basis of social characteristics; if, for example, a child has Asperger's syndrome, then he does not desire to socialize. However, as we have seen, these children want desperately to socialize; *they just don't know how.* Dr. Fred Volkmar recognizes the deep need for social acceptance on the part of many Asperger's children: "These are kids who have strong desire to make relationships. Who want to fit in. Who want to have friends...and who over and over again have the repeated experience of failure. Because they're not able to bring it off."[46] Asperger himself noted that the deficits in communication, especially in reciprocal communication, gravely affect the Asperger's syndrome child. These deficits lead to isolation and despair since the Asperger's syndrome child often does not understand how to initiate or conduct a social interaction using the rules most people regard as innate. Dr. Lorna Wing describes this exact difficulty, saying that they "make active but odd approaches to other people.... They pay no attention to the feelings or needs of other people they talk to. Some have poor eye contact, but the problem is usually timing of making and breaking eye contact rather than of avoidance.... Their approaches can include physically holding or hugging the other person, often much too tightly."[47]

Thus an Asperger's syndrome child violates both the unwritten rules for joint communication and respecting another's personal space. Often these children will stand too close to a person, speak in a loud unmodulated voice, and interrupt or make remarks out of context. These violations lead to peer rejection as well as frustration and anger. The verbal abilities of these children and their active social approaches may mask "the fact that they have no real understanding of how to interact socially with other people."[48] This makes diagnosis difficult since one of the main characteristics of Asperger's syndrome is impaired joint communication that arises not from the willful disregard of another person but "from a lack of ability to understand and use the rules governing social behavior."[49]

Just as we saw with their assessments of communication problems, ADHD researchers frequently regard the social difficulties of ADHD children as willful, conscious behaviors. For example, in his book *Taking Charge of ADHD,* Dr. Russell Barkley claims that "because [ADHD children] fail to consider future consequences, they often don't see that their selfishness and self-centeredness in the moment result in their losing friends in the long run."[50] What emerges from this perspective is a view of the ADHD child as one who has the capacity to learn social behaviors and to interpret social cues but who chooses to ignore the appropriate responses in lieu of immediate gratification. This approach implies that aberrant social behaviors emerge as a result of choice, even though Dr. Barkley argues that the impulsivity is evidence of a deficit in the behavioral inhibition system.[51] As a mother, my question becomes "How can researchers claim that a social behavior emerges from a biological impairment and, at the same time, assert that the behavior is willful and selfish?" Close examination reveals this same conflict in all major types of behavior discussed within the realm of ADHD.

I'M NOT BAD, JUST OUT OF CONTROL: SIMILARITIES IN BEHAVIOR

As we mentioned earlier, a diagnosis of ADHD often is accompanied by a co-morbid diagnosis of ODD or of conduct disorder. All of these disorders fall under the same category of attention-deficit and disruptive behavior disorders. Often the co-morbid diagnosis arises because the major diagnostic tool for ADHD is a behavioral checklist that focuses upon the child's willingness to comply with the demands of teachers and parents. Consequently, if a child does not comply or refuses to acknowledge the authority of the adult in control, then the child is often given a diagnosis of ODD. A recent article in *HealthWatch* claims that "about half the children diagnosed with ADHD also have oppositional defiant disorder."[52] More specifically, one study estimates the co-morbidity of ADHD and ODD as 65 percent.[53]

Interestingly, ODD behaviors are included in Conners' Rating Scale—a major diagnostic tool used to screen for ADHD. (See chapter 4 for more information on Conners' Scale.) Many of the defiant behaviors associated with ODD have long been recognized as part of Asperger's syndrome by researchers in autism but have not been labeled as a separate disorder. (In fact, Dr. Peter Tanguay once expressed to me that he would lobby to remove the ODD label because he believes it assigns intent to what is frequently recognized as behavior common to Asperger's syndrome patients.)

The DSM-IV-TR defines ODD as "a recurrent pattern of negativistic, defiant, disobedient and hostile behavior toward authority figures that persists for at least 6 months and is characterized by the frequent occurrence of at least four of the following behaviors: losing temper...arguing with adults...actively defying or refusing to comply with the requests or rules of adults...deliberately doing things that will annoy other people...blaming others for his or her own mistakes or behavior ...being touchy or easily annoyed by others ...being angry and resentful...or being spiteful or vindictive."[54]

Some of the accompanying tendencies that mark ODD include stubbornness, defiance, arguing, ignoring rules, hostile behaviors, temper tantrums, and an unwillingness to compromise. However, when these tendencies are combined with the impulsivity and inattention of ADHD, then the stage is set for a child to be seen as willfully disobedient, disruptive, defiant, explosive, unyielding, selfish, and self-centered—all adjectives used to describe ADHD and Asperger's syndrome children.

Several responses posted to Oprah Winfrey's show "Explosive Children" illustrate some profiles of children who fit this pattern of behavior. One mother blamed herself for her child's defiant behavior: "How does my son get rid of the anger that is inside of him? And WHY is that anger there? Did I do something wrong when he was a baby? Did I not seek help soon enough? How can he be so violent one minute and then the next, one of the most loving children I know?" Another parent wrote of her eight-year-old: "Any parent who has experienced firsthand the explosive rage attacks (these are NOT temper tantrums)...and known how much MORE terrible the child himself must feel than those who are watching him or her, knows this is not a simple behavior-mod issue and things cannot be changed through 'talk therapy.' " Yet another parent acknowledged having tried everything—"positive reinforcement charts, time outs, holding, calm communication." She was "tired of being judged...by society."[55] In other words, all of these parents have approached their child's oppositional behavior as something that can be modified by teaching appropriate behavioral responses through punishment and reward rather than as seeing the behavior as "an attempt to navigate in a world they are not equipped to fathom."[56]

Recent research in treatments for ADHD and ODD focuses primarily upon the symptoms of aggression, explosiveness, and defiance. Drs. Russell Barkley and Art Robin, experts in the ADHD field, have developed approaches to managing the disruptive behavior of these children, but these approaches are grounded in the assumption that ODD is a separate disorder from ADHD. This assumption is clearly illustrated in the following exchange taken from Robin's book *ADHD in Adolescents:*

> Mrs. Jones: This Oppositional Defiant Disorder thing. Is there a medication for that too?
>
> Dr. Robin: Not really. ADHD is thought to have a genetic/biological basis, but Oppositional Defiant Disorder is really good old learned bad habits. We will work together to try to teach Bill new ways of interacting with you, and [the] two of you new ways of interacting with him.[57]

From this passage you can see again that while these researchers contend that the behaviors in ADHD result from deficits in central inhibition control, at the same time they ascribe to the child a level of willfulness or an ability to manage the behavior. It is this inherent notion of willfulness that creates an image of the ADHD/ODD child as deliberate in her or his behaviors. This inherent notion gives rise to the idea that these children are bad. This inherent notion led at one time to a Web site like www.badkids.com for parents who had come to believe that their children were fundamentally flawed. And this inherent notion leads parents to believe they are failures.

In keeping with the idea that ODD is a learned behavior that occurs co-morbidly with ADHD, Drs. Barkley and Robin detail approaches for parents to prevent defiant explosive episodes. Barkley advocates behavior management and motivational approaches such as positive reinforcement and reward/punishment to develop a child's concept of time and consequence—two concepts that he claims are impaired in the ADHD/ODD child. Underlying this approach, however, are some core assumptions that give rise to the idea of the ADHD/ODD child as willful and the parents as weak. As Ross W. Greene explains, the first assumption "is that somewhere along the line, noncompliant children have learned that their tantrums, explosions, and destructiveness bring them attention or help them get their way by coercing...their parents to give in."[58] This assumption fuels the idea that the child's behavior "is planned, intentional, purposeful, and under the child's conscious control."[59] A logical result of this line of reasoning then becomes that the parents, too, are weak or out of control—a belief that causes professionals to blame parents and parents to blame themselves.

For years this approach has dominated ADHD literature and

research. Granted, the principles of consistent parenting through positive reinforcement and motivation are the hallmarks of effective parenting practices; however, the fundamental belief that an ADHD/ODD child can learn to diffuse the explosive behavior by applying the time and consequence theory assumes that the child can create goal-directed behavior, shift attention easily, regulate impulsive responses, and use reasoning, foresight, and premeditation to solve problems. Yet as Drs. Eric Courchene, Fred Volkmar, and Ami Klin—as well as numerous other researchers in autism—assert, children with impairments in the executive function have:

- the inability to plan and prioritize—they are impaired in their ability to set goals and prioritize activities to reach goals or solve problems
- the inability to assign attention to competing stimuli—they have difficulty with shifting attention or attending to more than one stimulus at a time
- poor temporal judgment—their ability to predict consequences through time is impaired
- weak organization skills[60]

We've seen the autism research explain this inability to inhibit responses and thereby respond purposively in a social environment as the result of a deficit or an impairment of the executive function. Consequently, while autism research also addresses the explosive tantrums and defiance of Asperger's syndrome children, *it accounts for this behavior biologically*—that is to say that the behavior has a biological basis, because it stems from a deficit that impairs the child's ability to respond normally to common situations.

It is important to note that both ADHD and autism research begin at the same biological place: a deficient executive function. However, rather than pursuing the same paths to explore origin and treatment, ADHD and autism have historically gone in different directions, especially in regard to behavior. As a result, ADHD has focused its efforts primarily upon behavioral modification, even though it is clear from the biology underlying this disorder that such modification will do little to address the fundamental deficits in the executive function. Autism, however, approaches behavior as part of the deficit rather than as a separate issue. Consequently, professionals in autism recognize that the concepts of time and consequence cannot be taught to a child with an autistic spectrum disorder. Instead, such concepts must be melded into a total framework of treatment, which includes aspects of behavior modification but does not solely rely upon it to mitigate oppositional behavior.

YOU SAY TO-MAY-TO, I SAY TO-MAH-TO: SIMILARITIES IN BEHAVIORAL RESPONSES

An inability to transition smoothly from one activity to another leads to a tantrum. Being in a loud noisy environment leads to agitation, distraction, and odd behavior. An affectionate touch causes a child to spin out of control. Each of these behavioral responses to the social environment is typical of both autism and ADHD. Often what parents and professionals are seeing as oppositional or defiant behavior is actually a child's attempt to protect himself or herself from intrusion or change. This characteristic arises not from a desire to control others but rather from a need to avoid being controlled or thrust into situations where the lack of communicative and social comprehension puts the child at the mercy of the environment.[61] Note in Table 3.1 that tantrums appear on both autism and ADHD's checklists for behaviors.

However, it is imperative to note that autism sees tantrum throwing as a natural response to the everyday demands of life placed upon the child, but ADHD views tantrum throwing as evidence of oppositional defiant behavior—thereby contributing to the ODD diagnosis.

A basic cause of tantrums is related to a rigid need for consistency and sameness. One of the first researchers in autism, Leo Kanner, noted that his patients were very much tethered to routine. In his paper "Autistic Disturbances of Affective Contact," Dr. Kanner calls this need for a highly structured routine an "autistic insistence upon sameness."[62] He observed in his research that autistic children are quite limited in their ability to tolerate spontaneity. In fact, Dr. Kanner states, "The child's behavior is governed by an anxiously obsessive desire for the maintenance of sameness that nobody but the child himself may disrupt on rare occasions." He cites instances where children would go into panic tantrums when furniture was rearranged, everyday routes were varied, or ritualistic sequences of events were not followed.[63] I've even noticed this feature in Sam. Once, on the way to school, I took a route different from our usual one. Throughout the entire drive, he was terribly upset, yelling and crying. He didn't calm down until I parked the car. At this point we were in the school's parking lot, and his morning was restored to its usual routine. This insistence upon sameness also drives children to throw tantrums if schedules suddenly change or if someone intrudes upon their daily schedules.

Interestingly, this insistence upon sameness has been recognized in current ADHD research. And this insistence is also linked to tantrums. A recent *HealthWatch* article states, "As ADHD children grow and develop, parents discover that these children have a very difficult time adapting to even minor changes in routines, such as getting up in the morning, putting on shoes, eating new foods, or going to bed. Any shift in a situation can precipitate a strong and noisy response."[64] One mother of an ADHD child reported that she dreads the beginning of school because it means changes in her child's morning routine. "It's always the same battles for about a month into the new school year—getting him up, getting him dressed, getting him to school on time. After three years, you'd think I'd be used to the arguments or you'd think he would have adapted." Clearly, any unexpected change generates undue anxiety and explosive responses in ADHD children—a response identical to children with autistic spectrum disorders.

Another cause for tantrums addressed in autistic research is environmentally based. As we explained earlier in the chapter, researchers in autism have long noted that autistic children are highly sensitive to the sensory experiences of their environment—especially with regard to auditory and tactile stimulation. Large gatherings and noisy surroundings make it difficult for the autistic child to filter all of the stimuli. Thus they become overwhelmed and frustrated. For instance, Temple Grandin describes her experiences at home when her family would visit: "When I was a child, large noisy gatherings of relatives were overwhelming, and I would just lose control and throw temper tantrums." Likewise, she notes that if her classroom had been what we regard as normal today, she would have been completely lost: "I would have drowned in a cacophony of confusion if I had been in an open classroom with thirty students doing ten different things."[65] What Dr. Grandin describes is an inability to filter noises or to attend to only one stimulus in the midst of many. Needless to say, such confusion would easily lead to a tantrum in a child. Her response when she was young was the typical response for autistic and ADHD children worldwide—to throw a tantrum.

Like their autistic counterparts, ADHD children are hypersensitive to busy surroundings such as malls or noisy classrooms. Such environments overstimulate ADHD children and, according to a recent *Health-Watch* article, "cause them to become distracted and react by pulling items off the shelves, hitting people, or spinning out of control into erratic, silly, or strange behavior."[66] Another mother tells of how she deliberately schedules her shopping trips to avoid taking her ADHD child. "He gets all worked up when we're in crowded places. He becomes angry and hard to control. I've walked out of stores and left full carts because he acts so bad."

Finally, another common cause of tantrums is the hostile response to tactile stimulation. As we said earlier, both autism and ADHD researchers have recognized that children with these disorders are acutely sensitive to touch. Autistic children experience hypersensitivity to showers, hair washing, clothing, and hugging. Similarly, ADHD children are hypersensitive to tactile stimulation and often try to avoid uncomfortable sensations. This oversensitivity leads to aggressive responses such as pulling away abruptly from people and hitting others. Such responses may appear to stem from anger but actually arise from a child's inability to endure overstimulation.

WHERE DO WE GO FROM HERE?

When the ADHD child seeks to avoid or reacts to protect himself from the sensory stimuli or changes in environment, he is labeled by the ADHD perspective as defiant, willful, and oppositional. This same child, when seen through the lens of autistic research, is understood as one who throws tantrums because of a biological deficit that impairs his ability to filter sensory stimuli and respond to changes in his social environment.

Although recent research in both fields suggests that autistic spectrum disorders and ADHD fundamentally share the same origin, the same characteristics, and the same manifestations in communication, social interaction and behavior, the DSM-IV-TR and researchers still insist that these are totally distinct disorders. As a mother searching for diagnosis and treatment options, I wonder if the solution could be as simple as researchers from both sides stopping long enough to compare notes and collectively examine these disorders. Until then, we'll need to press forward in fully informing ourselves for the sake of our children.

Chapter 4

The Problem with Current Diagnostic Practices

How ADHD Screening Tools Lend Themselves to Misdiagnosis

> *What does it mean when we say "two disorders are different"? Different at the level of simple symptoms and behaviors or different at a more fundamental level of mechanism and process?... Indeed, will it ever be possible to decide whether two disorders are the same or different in the absence of perfectly conclusive evidence? As a result of these and other considerations, I argue that for some distinctions it is more important to evaluate the usefulness of diagnostic distinctions rather than their validity.*
>
> PETER SZATMARI

Dr. David J. Kupfer, Thomas Detre Professor and Chair at the University of Pittsburgh's Department of Psychiatry, recently made the following statement regarding the level of care that ADHD children receive:

> Children with ADHD often receive an inconsistent level of care from a fragmented system that consumes a large share of health care dollars.... There is no consistency in treatment, diagnosis or follow-up for children with ADHD. It is a major public health problem. The problem is compounded by the fact that an accurate diagnosis for ADHD remains elusive and controversial yet continues to be a commonly diagnosed behavioral disorder of childhood.[1]

Needless to say this statement did little to reassure anxious parents, especially those deeply invested in the ADHD system, because all treatment hinges upon obtaining a timely, accurate diagnosis and impacts a child for a lifetime. Early intervention and treatment affect a child's development dramatically, especially in terms of communication, behavior, and social integration.

SUBJECTIVITY: THE MAIN ROADBLOCK TO EARLY INTERVENTION

The American Academy of Pediatrics recently issued guidelines for diagnosing ADHD. Specifically, pediatricians are encouraged to

- evaluate children six to twelve years of age who present with inattention, hyperactivity, impulsivity, academic underachievement, or behavior problems
- use DSM-IV-TR criteria in establishing the diagnosis
- obtain information about core symptoms, age of onset, duration of symptoms, and degree of impairment directly from parents/caregivers

- obtain information directly from classroom teachers about core symptoms, age of onset, duration of symptoms, degree of impairment, and coexisting conditions
- assess the children they diagnose with ADHD for coexisting conditions

These guidelines are troublesome for several reasons. First, the initial recommendation is for primary care physicians to evaluate *only* for ADHD (i.e., not autism as well) when children ages six to twelve present with symptoms of hyperactivity, impulsivity, and inattention as well as behavioral problems.[2] Moreover, physicians are also encouraged to screen routinely for ADHD during regular health exams. As a result of this insistence upon ADHD screening, a child who presents with these symptoms is more likely to be pigeonholed into this disorder rather than to be simultaneously screened for autism; as I've already pointed out, most physicians are unaware of the similarities between Asperger's syndrome and ADHD, especially in terms of symptoms.

Second, while screening a child for ADHD, the AAP recommends physicians assess for co-morbid conditions such as anxiety problems, mood disorder, and conduct problems—specifically oppositional defiant disorder.[3] This, of course, will make the diagnosis of ADHD more complex and at the same time more certain, since, as discussed in chapter 3, ODD is generally thought to go hand-in-hand with attention deficit disorder. In *Diagnostic Options in Autism: A Guide for Professionals,* one of the central behavioral concerns for *autism assessment* is whether the child is uncooperative or oppositional as well as hyperactive.[4] It is clear that ADHD and autism share similar diagnostic characteristics. Nevertheless, because the AAP encourages physicians to screen for ADHD, and because ADHD receives so much publicity from the media and the pharmaceutical companies, if a child presents with symptoms of hyperactivity and oppositional behavior, the odds are that the child will receive a diagnosis of ADHD with ODD, even though autism might be the more accurate diagnosis.

Third, the AAP strongly recommends that assessment for and diagnosis of ADHD derive primarily from observations made by parents or caregivers and teachers. These observations should present evidence about the core symptoms of ADHD in various settings, the age of onset, duration of symptoms, and the degree of functional impairment. Specifically, "open-ended questions (e.g., 'What are your concerns about your child's behavior in school?'), focused questions regarding particular behaviors, semi-structured interview schedules, questionnaires and rating scales" are the primary tools for this type of assessment.[5]

To this end, the Conners' Rating Scales for parents and teachers are the standard for ADHD evaluation. Some of the more common ADHD rating scales are the Conners' Parent Rating Scale, 1997 (CPRS-R: L-ADHD), the Conners' Teacher Rating Scale, 1997 (CTRS-R: L-ADHD), and the Child Behavior Checklist (CBCL). Each of these checklists relies upon direct observation and feedback from parents/caregivers and teachers to evaluate a child for ADHD. While these scales assess how a child adapts to the school environment, they also focus upon behavioral problems, conduct problems, hyperactivity, inattention-passivity, and aggression. In other words, these rating scales gather data based upon subjective opinion and observation to screen for behavior problems in addition to the symptoms of hyperactivity, impulsivity, and inattention.

Essentially, these rating scales not only screen for the core symptoms of ADHD but also provide a convenient vehicle for diagnosing a child with ODD or even CD. Such multiple diagnoses, especially if they are not accurate, can complicate treatment and impact a child's emotional, mental, and physical development. When Sam was evaluated for ADHD, one examiner stated that he "sees a combination of the early Attention Deficit Hyperactivity Disorder and Oppositional Defiant Disorder of Childhood." He also added, "Young children with the Attention Deficit Hyperactivity Disorder are *very likely to develop specific levels of oppositional behavior*" (emphasis added). In other words, this physician not only saw ODD in Sam at age four but predicted that Sam would develop ODD as he matured.

At the same time the AAP calls for screening all children between six and twelve years old for ADHD, the American Academy of Neurology and the Child Neurology Society urge a "routine developmental surveillance and screening specifically for autism to be performed on all children," preferably during the toddler to preschool years.[6] Sadly, the diagnosis of autism often is not made until two to three years after parents first notice the symptoms. For children with Asperger's syndrome, a diagnosis, if obtained, is rarely given before age six.

Like ADHD experts, autism experts rely upon rating scales and direct observation when assessing a child. The Childhood Autism Rating Scale and the High-Functioning Autism Spectrum Screening Questionnaire rely upon feedback from healthcare professionals, teachers, and parents to diagnose behaviors commonly associated with autism. As Table 3.1 illustrated (see chapter 3), many of the behaviors are common to both Asperger's syndrome and ADHD. Involuntary or nervous body movements are listed on all of the rating scales and may be interpreted as hyperactivity. Resistance to change, special routines, and being fearful or quarrelsome are also common symptoms on the scales and are often interpreted as oppositional defiance by ADHD diagnosticians. As you can probably guess by now, professionals in autism recognize that these behaviors are a response to the autistic insistence upon sameness and are not willfully aggressive responses. Likewise, the speech and language issues listed on the checklists may differ in terms of level and degree, but all indicate an underlying communication disorder. Again, ADHD research attributes speech issues to impulsivity, while the autism field views these behaviors through the lens of impaired reciprocal communications. *Thus, it is easy to see how difficult it is to differentiate between these disorders solely upon the basis of observation, opinion, and behaviors.*

Autism experts recognize that diagnosing a child on the basis of behaviors alone leads to misdiagnosis, especially in the case of Asperger's syndrome. For one, these children appear more capable than children with classic autism. Also, pediatricians are instructed to look for ADHD rather than consider the symptoms within an autistic framework. Misdiagnosed children lose valuable time and opportunity for early intervention and treatment.

Dr. Diane Twachtman-Cullen writes that because these children "present a somewhat enigmatic picture behaviorally, they are often misdiagnosed. Labels such as 'Oppositional Disorder' [and] Conduct Disorder [CD]...are often used to describe individuals who would clearly fit the clinical picture of Asperger Syndrome." More importantly, however, she articulates the essential dilemma with these labels: Because they are emotionally and/or psychiatrically based, "they do not recognize the neurological basis for the symptomatology.... Worse yet, they often give the impression that the aberrant behavior associated with the disorder is willful and volitional, as opposed to that which results from a neurologically compromised system."[7]

Clearly, when an area of science relies principally upon subjective data such as observation and opinion, the validity of its findings is questionable. The AAP recognizes the limitations of current ADHD diagnostic methods, especially when "the behaviors used in making a DSM-IV diagnosis fall on a spectrum,"[8] thereby making exact diagnosis quite difficult. However, the fact remains that ADHD as a disorder relies mainly upon behavior as its central underpinning. The DSM-IV-TR criteria are all behaviorally based, the screening and diagnostic process focuses upon behavior, and the treatments are primarily centered around behavior modification. Yet approximately twelve million adults[9] and 3 to 7 percent of school-age children are diagnosed with ADHD using these clinically questionable methods.

At the bottom line, ADHD as a science is grounded in subjective opinion about people's behaviors rather than having a proven pathological basis like other disorders or diseases. It is this very issue that the National Institute of Mental Health (NIMH) recognized when it convened a group of clinical and research scientists to identify potential areas of collaborative research into ADHD. In particular, the NIMH meeting focused upon how scientists from areas such as neuroscience, biology, cognitive psychology, and genetics could collaborate to help establish the central characteristics, origins, and symptoms of ADHD. The NIMH clearly identified the need for ADHD to be grounded in hard science, saying that while "ADHD is conceptualized as a cognitive deficit…its DSM-IV symptoms are described by their behavioral manifestation."[10] During this meeting, "a need was identified for scientists to translate basic science findings for application to the underlying causes of ADHD, differential diagnosis, as well as implications for targeted prevention and treatment."[11] The scientific disciplines that the NIMH listed for collaboration are neuroscience as well as the biological and cognitive sciences.

GENETIC RESEARCH: WHERE AUTISM EXPERTS LEAD THE WAY

Interestingly, these are the principal areas in which autism research focuses in its search for causes, symptomatology, and treatments for the behaviors associated with autistic spectrum disorders. Major university-based projects such as Stanford's Autism Genetic Research Program[12] have been fortified and expanded with collaborative multi-site grants such as Research Units on Pediatric Psychopharmacology (RUPP)[13] and the Collaborative Autism Project (CAP).[14] These collaborations have added monumentally to the advances in understanding the nature of human development. However, they are by no means the only sites now actively doing this kind of research. Duke University,[15] the Yale Child Study Center,[16] the Seaver Center at Mount Sinai,[17] the University of Pittsburgh, Baylor University, the University of Rochester, and a host of other research facilities have joined in the hunt as well.

It is worth noting that many of the subjects of research covered in autism are becoming the newest and hottest areas in ADHD research or are subjects that ADHD researchers have explored but not to the extent that autism researchers have. What emerges, then, is an overlap between autism and ADHD research with the autism camp leading the way in terms of reliability and the hard science that the NIMH wants from the ADHD field. Specifically, the areas of overlap are in research upon genetic markers and causes of the disorders, the absence of essential fatty acids, neurotransmitters, and cognitive processing.

Autism researchers have always been aware of the genetic/inherited nature of the disorder. Evidence indicates that autism is approximately 90 percent inheritable.[18] It is commonly recognized that a parent or grandparent with Asperger's syndrome or autism will produce descendants with the disorder. It is also commonly recognized that if parents have one child with autism, their chances of having another child with the disorder are increased. Additionally, evidence suggests that unaffected family members may share with the affected family member genes that predispose them for milder behavioral characteristics that are similar to those of autism.[19] For example, some relatives of people with autism may have mild social, language, or reading problems. Family members also may share telltale neurochemical signatures that may be implicated in the disorder.[20] Researchers are studying such families to characterize these behavioral and biological traits in hopes of tracing the variations in the genetic blueprint that contribute to autism.

Recent research has gone even further into the genetic causes of autism; now, specific chromosomes are believed to be a factor in autism. In fact, the NIMH press release "Brain Gene Implicated in Autism" details one specific chromosome and gene that researchers believe are responsible: "They pinpointed the candidate gene, WNT2, in a region of chromosome 7 [where] rare mutations in WNT2 may 'significantly increase susceptibility to autism...while a common variant may contribute to the disorder to a lesser degree.' "[21] An article in the *American Journal of Human Genetics* reports on tests of siblings to identify regions of linkage. Chromosome 7q as well as chromosome 16p were implicated as regions of susceptibility.[22] Drs. Flavio Keller and Antonio Persico have announced the discovery of a gene that may increase threefold a child's risk of being diagnosed with autism. The gene, which produces the protein reelin, has recently been associated with bipolar disorder and schizophrenia. However, unlike many developmental genes, the reelin gene continues to be expressed throughout life, potentially giving the pharmaceutical industry its first "target" for an autism medication.[23] Studies such as these offer much hope and only scratch the surface of what scientists expect to discover about autism and its related disorders through genetic research. "Geneticists estimate as many as 15 different genes may put children at risk of developing autism."[24]

ADHD researchers are only just beginning to look at the genetic basis for the disorder. Like autism, ADHD is recognized as inheritable; parents with ADHD are the most likely to produce children with ADHD: "Studies have identified the most common etiology to be hereditary [and] reveal that 75% of the statistical variance between those with ADHD and normative samples can be attributed to genetic factors. There is also an increased risk for ADHD in first-degree relatives."[25] However, ADHD research has yet to go as far as autism in search of chromosomal regions that may increase susceptibility.

In addition to attempting to establish a genetic cause for autism, researchers have explored the role that neurotransmitters such as dopamine and serotonin play in autism as well as ADHD. Table 4.1 illustrates the common neurotransmitter, its gene, and the disease with which each is most frequently associated. Although both autism and ADHD claim bipolar disorder as a co-morbid condition exclusive to themselves, notice the frequency with which disease associations list all three for shared genes and neurotransmitters. Yet, while autism recognizes that ADHD may be a co-morbid condition, ADHD does not recognize autism in the same way. Thus, the genetic causes underlying autism appear to be strongly shared with ADHD. Another possible marker for autism and ADHD relates to essential fatty acids. Low levels of these acids have been linked to neurodevelopmental and psychiatric disorders such as ADHD, autism, bipolar disorder, dyspraxia, and dyslexia.

Given the explorations into co-morbid conditions and genetic and biological markers, it is easy to see how autism researchers are searching for the neurological basis of the behaviors addressed in the Childhood

Table 4.1 The Common Neurotransmitter, Gene, and Associated Diseases[26]

NEURO-TRANSMITTER	GENE(i)	DISEASE ASSOCIATIONS(ii)	EFFECT OF MUTATIONS
Serotonin	5-HTT(iii) serotonin transporter 17q11.1-12	ADHD, Autism(iv), BP(v)	Polymorphism leading to increased uptake of serotonin and a decrease in activity Polymorphism in promoter may lead to reduced transcription
Serotonin	TPH tryptophan-hydroxylase 11p15.3-p14	Autism(vi), BP(vii)	Association between TPH mutation and suicide (inconclusive) Mutation in nearby HRAS-1 may affect TPH
Serotonin	5HTR2A post-synaptic serotonin receptor 5-HT_2 13q14-q21	ADHD, Autism(viii), BP	Decreased 5-HT_2 binding plays a rôle in aggression and anxiety Mutant form of regulatory gene could result in fewer receptors and binding opportunities
Dopamine	DRD2 dopamine receptor D2 11q23	ADHD(ix), Autism(x)	Exact polymorphism unknown; mutation likely to result in decreased dopaminergic activity
Dopamine	DRD4(xi) dopamine receptor D4 11p15.5	ADHD(xii), BP(xiii)	Null mutation results in a truncated non-functional protein and a decrease in dopaminergic activity 7-repeat allele leads to an increase of novelty seeking

Table 4.1 The Common Neurotransmitter, Gene, and Associated Diseases (continued)

NEURO-TRANSMITTER	GENE(i)	DISEASE ASSOCIATIONS(ii)	EFFECT OF MUTATIONS
Dopamine	DRD5 dopamine receptor D5 4p16.1-p15.3	ADHD, Autism(xiv)	Exact polymorphism unknown; mutation likely to result in decreased dopaminergic activity
Dopamine	DAT1 dopamine transporter 5p15.3	ADHD(xv), Autism, BP(xvi)	480-bp polymorphism is highly associated with decreased dopamine transporter functioning
Dopamine	TH tyrosine hydroxylase 11p15.5	ADHD(xvii), Autism, BP(xviii)	Allele 2 may be linked to mild depression, often seen in all three disorders Disruption in activity could lessen both dopamine and norepinephrine levels
Noradrenaline (Norepine-phrine)	DβH dopamine β hydroxylase 9q34	ADHD(xix)	Lack of functional DβH results in low levels of noradrenaline, therefore less NA activity
Noradrenaline (Norepine-phrine)	ADRA2 α2-adrenergic receptor 10q24-q26	ADHD(xx)	Some drugs known to alleviate symptoms have been shown to increase firing of NA neurons. Thus, symptoms of ADHD may appear due to decreased firing of locus coeruleus.

Autism Rating Scale (CARS) and the High-Functioning Autism Spectrum Screening Questionnaire (see Table 4.2). Autism recognizes that the behaviors are not the end of the diagnostic journey; rather, they are the manifestations of a disorder that is biological in origin. Consequently, as autism researchers look for ways to more accurately diagnose and assess patients at a younger age, they look to the hard sciences to identify the core variables of the disorder.

Because ADHD focuses primarily upon the behaviors as the core disorder, what emerges is a disorder that promotes "chasing behavior problems—that is, constantly altering...treatments and redesignating target behaviors" rather than exploring the hard science beneath the disorder.[27] Sadly, ADHD has become the most frequently diagnosed disorder of childhood. Our pediatricians are instructed to screen for ADHD and then must rely upon checklists and rating scales that are vague and generate primarily subjective data. Yet what is truly frightening is that when a child presents with symptoms of Asperger's syndrome, he will most certainly receive a diagnosis of ADHD, because autism is not a choice. And because autism is not a diagnostic choice, neither is proper, essential, and immediate treatment.

Table 4.2 Comparing Rating Scales of Autism and ADHD

CHILDHOOD AUTISM RATING SCALE[28]	CONNERS' PARENT QUESTIONNAIRE FOR ADHD CHILDREN[29]
Behaviors that are clearly strange or unusual for a child may include finger movements, peculiar finger or body posturing, staring or picking at the body, self-directed aggression, rocking, spinning, finger wiggling, or toe walking.	Picks at things (nails, fingers, hair, clothing) Sucks or chews (thumb, clothing, blankets) Destructive
Abnormal adaptation to change. The child actively resists change in routine, tries to continue old activities, and is difficult to distract. He or she may become angry and unhappy when an established routine is altered.	Fearful (of new situations, new people or places, going to school) Quarrelsome Mood changes quickly and drastically Disobedient or obeys reluctantly Has difficulty learning Sassy to grownups Denies mistakes or blames others Wants to run things

Child Behavior Checklist (ADHD)[30]	The High-Functioning Autism Spectrum Screening Questionnaire[31]
Deliberately harms self or attempts suicide Destroys his/her own things Destroys things belonging to his/her family or others Bites fingernails Sucks thumb Moves or twitches nervously	Has involuntary face and body movements Has markedly unusual facial expression Has markedly unusual posture
Argues a lot Disobedient at school and at home Fears certain animals, situations, or places, other than school Fears going to school Fears he/she might think or do something bad Doesn't seem to feel guilty after misbehaving Feels too guilty Too fearful or anxious Too concerned with neatness or cleanliness Sudden changes in mood or feelings Suspicious Can't sit still, restless, hyperactive Nervous, high-strung or tense Impulsive or acts without thinking Underactive, slow moving, or lacks energy Lies or cheats Sets fires Steals at home Steals outside the home Vandalizes Brags and boasts	Has special routines: insists on no change Shows idiosyncratic attachment to objects Lacks empathy Lacks common sense

Table 4.2 Comparing Rating Scales of Autism and ADHD (continued)

CHILDHOOD AUTISM RATING SCALE	CONNERS' PARENT QUESTIONNAIRE FOR ADHD CHILDREN
Persistent and forceful attempts are necessary to get the child's attention at times. Minimal contact initiated by the child	Distractability or attention-span problems Daydreams
When present, verbal communication may be a mixture of some meaningful speech and some peculiar speech such as jargon, echolalia, or pronoun reversal. Peculiarities in meaningful speech include excessive questioning or preoccupation with particular topics.	Speaks differently from others his/her own age (baby talk, stuttering, is hard to understand)
	Fails to finish things Easily frustrated in efforts
	Disturbs other children Gets into trouble more than others of the same age Lets self get pushed around Problems with making or keeping friends

CHILD BEHAVIOR CHECKLIST (ADHD)	THE HIGH-FUNCTIONING AUTISM SPECTRUM SCREENING QUESTIONNAIRE
Can't concentrate, can't pay attention for long periods of time Can't get his/her mind off certain thoughts; obsessions Clings to adults or is too dependent Demands a lot of attention Would rather be alone than with others Shy or timid Stares blankly Prefers being with older or younger children Confused or seems to be in a fog Daydreams or gets lost in his/her own thoughts	Lives somewhat in a world of his/her own with restricted idiosyncratic intellectual interests Can be with other children but only on his/her terms Has a deviant style gaze
Unusually loud Talks too much Secretive, keeps things to self Sees things that aren't there	Has a literal understanding of ambiguous and metaphorical language Has a deviant style of communication with a formal, fussy, old fashioned, or "robotlike" language Invents idiosyncratic words and expressions Has different voice or speech Expresses sounds voluntarily; clears throat, grunts, smacks, cries, or screams
Feels he/she has to be perfect Poor schoolwork Truant, skips school	Has difficulties in completing simple, daily activities because of compulsory repletion of certain actions or thoughts
Poor coordination or clumsy	Has clumsy, ill-coordinated, ungainly, awkward movements or gestures
Does not get along with other children Hangs around with others who get into trouble Not liked by other kids Teases a lot Threatens people Has temper tantrums or is hot tempered Shows off or clowns	Is bullied by other children Is surprisingly good at some things and surprisingly poor at others Is poor at games, no idea of cooperating in a team, scores "own" goals Makes naïve and embarrassing remarks

Chapter 5

The Changing Faces of Autism

Developmental Stages from Infancy to Adolescence

He has made everything beautiful in its time.

ECCLESIASTES 3:11

By now it's evident that autistic spectrum disorders and ADHD are disorders of development—that is, they manifest themselves differently at different ages and in different people. This is why researchers often see one set of symptoms or behaviors at a certain age and call it ADHD. However, in a few years new symptoms and behaviors emerge and—wonder of wonders—the patient in question receives a new diagnosis. Consequently, children often end up with several differential diagnoses by the time they're through their teenage years. A clearer understanding of this dynamic process may also help avoid misdiagnoses. (See Table 5.1 for a summary of how the disorders manifest themselves at different developmental stages and when they are usually diagnosed.)

Table 5.1: Manifestation of Disorders at Different Developmental Stages and When They Are Usually Diagnosed

	AUTISM	ASPERGER'S SYNDROME	ADHD
Birth to 3 years	Children are diagnosed before the age of three. **Social:** Significant impairments in social interaction **Communication:** Impairments in communication (language delay) **Behavior:** Behavior impairments (restricted/repetitive)	No clinically significant delay in early language	Not typically diagnosed because there is little known about ADHD in these age groups
3 to 6 years		Children may be initially diagnosed. Very little, if any, language delay. Asperger's children usually have a well-developed vocabulary; however, they often misuse words because they do not understand the meaning or the pragmatics (the application of language).	Not typically diagnosed because there is little known about ADHD in these age groups

Table 5.1: Manifestation of Disorders at Different Developmental Stages and When They Are Usually Diagnosed (continued)

	AUTISM	ASPERGER'S SYNDROME	ADHD
6 to 12 years		Children who appear to have normal language development are often not recognized until school age. **Social:** Impairments in social interaction. Social deficits are often masked by strong verbal skills. **Communication:** Strengths in verbal ability (vocabulary and rote auditory memory). Weakness in nonverbal areas, i.e., motor clumsiness and awkwardness (visual/motor and visual/spatial). **Behavior:** Symptoms of inattention and overactivity (hyperactivity) are present. Many receive a diagnosis of ADHD prior to the diagnosis of Asperger's. Good verbal skills lead teachers and caregivers to attribute behavior difficulties to willfulness or stubbornness.	Children are often diagnosed after they enter the school setting. **Social:** They have a difficult time making and maintaining friendships. Interference with developmentally appropriate social functioning. **Communication:** Inattention is attributed to not following the rules of social interaction (playground activities and conversation). **Behavior:** Symptoms of inattention, overactivity/hyperactivity, and distractibility. Frequently interrupt, intrude, and are impatient in social settings. Varying symptoms often lead others to believe that all the troublesome behavior is willful.

Table 5.1: Manifestation of Disorders at Different Developmental Stages and When They Are Usually Diagnosed (continued)

	AUTISM	ASPERGER'S SYNDROME	ADHD
12 to 17 years		Social isolation and disabilities become more striking over time. Older individuals may have an *interest* in friendship but lack *understanding* of the rules of social interaction, resulting in peer rejection. Social isolation and self-awareness in adolescence can lead to depression and anxiety.	They often use their high IQ to compensate for various weaknesses. Adolescents struggle with low self-esteem and with depression.

INFANCY THROUGH AGE THREE

During this period of a child's development, joint communication, language acquisition, and interaction/intimacy are three developmental markers noted in autism literature. In his wonderful book *The Child with Special Needs,* Stanley Greenspan details several milestones that children must master to move to the next stage of development. Some of the most common milestones recognizable to parents of infants with autistic spectrum disorders include sensory/self-regulation, intimacy, joint communication, and complex communication. Unfortunately, parents usually recognize deficits in these areas only in hindsight—typically when a child is being screened for learning disabilities or ADHD.

Christopher was what everyone would call a "good" baby. Even in a household with two preschool-age siblings, Chris would lie quietly in his crib and never demanded attention. He never acknowledged his mother or sisters coming into or leaving a room. Likewise, his mother would make attempts to get his attention, especially during feedings, when she would try to make eye contact and initiate "baby" conversations. Chris would not respond. He would gaze off into space rather than watch his mother's mouth or react to his family's efforts to engage him. Accordingly, Chris did not begin speaking until he was thirty-four months old, even though doctors insisted his IQ was normal.

Rather than play with others, Chris preferred to play alone. His play was repetitive and imitative. Instead of rolling his cars across the floor or using them to create different scenarios, Chris would repetitively line up his cars in the same configuration as the cars in his sister's preschool carpool line. Whenever anyone would try to play along with him or break the configuration, Chris would throw a tantrum, destroy the pattern, and then reset it.

Clearly Chris's symptoms illustrate several deficiencies in development. His solitary play, language delay, and inability to communicate nonverbally all are typical of developmental disorders noted in autistic spectrum disorders. Medical professionals, however, did not consider autism as a possible diagnosis and instead treated his verbal and social delays as being within the normal range.

Like Chris, my son Sam was considered a child who developed "normally" during these first three years. However, Sam's development looked much more typical than Chris's; in fact, as far as appearances go, Sam looked like a little genius.

Sam was a verbally engaging baby. From six months on he used simple words to try to converse with his brothers and me. By twelve months he was talking in sentences. We never considered that he might not comprehend the meaning of his words. We assumed that since he used them, he understood them. Thus we thought of Sam as exceptionally social and intelligent.

We did notice oddities, however. Even though Sam would engage my husband or me verbally while we were in the room, he never took note of our entering or departing. He would not greet us or acknowledge us until we deliberately drew attention to ourselves, especially if he was playing. Similarly, Sam's play was nearly identical to Chris's. He played repetitively, reconstructing patterns he'd seen. Also, he would spend a lot of time arranging and rearranging his toys. We were amused by his "hyperorganization," thinking it was cute. Now, however, we realize that it, too, was a marker for Asperger's syndrome.

Interestingly, the very deficit in language that Chris illustrated would lead ADHD researchers to misdiagnose Sam. They assumed that because Sam's verbal skills were so advanced, he had no communication disorder. Likewise, up until the age of three, we thought Sam was an exceptional albeit "normal" child. We never suspected that he had any developmental delays—verbal or social.

AGES THREE THROUGH SIX

Throughout this developmental stage, children develop nonverbal communication skills that help them navigate socially in this world. Reading facial expressions, understanding taking turns in conversations, comprehending deeper meanings of language, sharing, interpreting body language—all of these abilities are necessary to function in the playground of life. Any deficits in these areas will cause extreme frustration in the child as well as in those with whom he interacts. It is usually at this stage of development that both Asperger's syndrome and ADHD begin to be recognized. The difficulty, as we have seen, is in obtaining an accurate diagnosis.

Ben, my middle son, was six years old when I first took him to Dr. John Lacey. Ben had always been cuddly and sweet as an infant, even though he was also content to sit in his swing for hours and not fuss or cry for attention. I though he was such a "good" baby. That's why, as he grew and began having difficulty with his peers, I couldn't understand the problem. Ben got along well with adults. In fact, when in a group of people, as at a birthday party, Ben would seek out the adults rather than stay with his peers. Another problem Ben had with socializing was black-and-white thinking and literal interpretations. To him, rules were made never to be broken; when his friends misbehaved, even in private, Ben would report the infraction. Needless to say, this made him extremely unpopular. Yet Ben could not understand why his friends would get angry.

During this stage of development, Ben also became more hyperactive

—or so it seemed. Perhaps this increase was simply more apparent in the classroom setting, which is where his hyperactivity was first noted. Ben would not stay seated, would continually jump up to sharpen his pencil, and would generally disrupt the class with his movements. His teacher claimed that Ben's behavior was willful and defiant.

Besides the problems with socializing and hyperactivity, the major problem that drove me to take Ben to Dr. Lacey was motor coordination. Because his social and motor skills were substandard and he was hyperactive, he received a diagnosis of ADHD without ODD. Dr. Lacey recommended stimulants to treat him. Our reluctance to try medications led us to try some of Dr. Barkley's behavior management techniques—positive reinforcement, time-outs, and punishment and rewards—all to no avail. Only when we felt like we'd reached a dead end did we turn to the medications, which worked wonderfully.

Around age three and a half, Sam's tantrums became unmanageable. He would lose his temper for no apparent reason. Any disruption or change in his routine brought on a tantrum. My day often began with Sam's hiding under his bed, screaming and grunting at me while refusing to go to preschool. Then, once at preschool, he would refuse to engage in activities that required a change in his own routine. If he was coloring and the group was going to the gym, he would throw a tantrum. When he went to the gym and settled in there, he would rage when he had to return to the room. When I came to take him home, he would have another fit. Needless to say, this became the norm for our interactions with Sam. Bath time, bedtime, church, school, play—any transition or change precipitated a violent response. And as he grew older, his behavior grew worse. Understandably, I felt like a horrible mother. My child wouldn't behave. I had to fight with him to get him to do anything. By all standards, I was a failure.

At the same time, though, Sam was the classic stereotype of the "Little Professor." We used to say that all he needed was the bow tie to complete his professorial image. His verbal and intellectual abilities were extraordinary. He took any new concept introduced to him and integrated it into his thinking immediately. For instance, when he was four years old, he asked me about the states of matter: gases, liquids, and solids. I explained about how almost everything in the world falls into one of these categories. Two days later, as he watched water boiling, he told me that water could fall under all three categories and gave me the examples of steam, water, and ice.

Sam taught himself to read from the back of cereal boxes. He had a vocabulary that constantly amazed us. We didn't realize that he didn't understand the meaning of what he said and read. After all, how could a child who acquired language so readily have problems with communication? But Sam did have problems with communication—the nonverbal type. He could not recognize facial expressions. Once he asked me outright if the expression I wore was my "mad face." He could not understand anything beyond the literal meaning of language. When we asked him about the meaning of what he had read, he had no comprehension. He was merely decoding the words. And when playing, he could not read the body language of his friends. Thus he could not tell when he was too rough, too close, or too loud. Basically, Sam could not communicate effectively at all.

Because Dr. Lacey had moved out of state, I took Sam to the Bingham Center for evaluation. Here he received a diagnosis of ADHD with ODD. I was told that his full-scale IQ of 143 put him in the gifted range. As a result, they told me that Sam was deliberately manipulating me—that his defiant behavior was willful, premeditated, and designed to gain his own end. I was told to use holding therapy during his tantrums and to visit twice weekly for play therapy to teach him social skills. I agreed to come for the play therapy but immediately rejected the notion of restraining Sam.

However, as his behavior grew worse with age, I sought out more professional help. I saw three more physicians, each independently perplexed by the degree and complexity of his condition, before Dr. Tanguay finally diagnosed Sam with Asperger's syndrome. His written analysis cleared up some of the confusion about Sam's behavior and social problems:

> Although social communication deficits once were identified as being especially noteworthy in persons diagnosed as having *infantile* autism, it has since been recognized that the deficits may present in milder forms in the general population, and that even a mild to moderate degree of such a deficit can turn out to be a serious problem. Among other things, these children may be thought to be willfully and inexplicably stubborn, insensitive to the feelings of others, selfish, or "spoiled rotten."

AGES SIX THROUGH TWELVE

Once children begin functioning in a school environment, both Asperger's syndrome and ADHD present themselves with nearly identical symptoms. This period of development is when most ADHD and ODD diagnoses are made, since behavior and social problems become most evident through the classroom setting. During this stage of development, symptoms of inattentiveness, hyperactivity, impulsivity, and difficulty making friends interfere with a child's relationships both in and out of school. Once again, the average to above-average verbal abilities of most Asperger's syndrome and ADHD children lead most professionals to attribute their behavioral and social problems to willfulness or stubbornness rather than to an inherent communication disorder.

Ben's hyperactivity really became a problem after age seven. Even though he was on Ritalin, his impulsivity and activity levels soared, especially outside of the classroom. For instance, in stores he would tear up and down the aisles and pull items off the shelves, not out of anger but out of overstimulation. Likewise, he would do things without thinking, like play with lighters or tell on his friends because they broke rules. Fortunately the Ritalin kept him focused enough on school tasks that learning was not an issue. In fact, once on the medication, he performed quite well academically.

But Ritalin did not help Ben with his social problems. He still had difficulties with peer relationships. Contrary to the prevalent theories in ADHD that the hyperactivity interfered with social relationships, Ben's problems stemmed from deficits in nonverbal communication. He had no perception of personal space, so he often sat too close to his friends, got too close to their faces when talking, or reached out to touch them at odd times. Likewise, because he could not understand personal boundaries, he would be too honest with his friends and consequently anger them; once again, he could not fathom why they were angry. Along these same lines, he would share too many secrets and would constantly make poor judgments about whom to trust. Another aspect of social difficulties stemmed from Ben's poor motor skills. He was extremely clumsy and awkward, so his peers didn't want to play with him.

Until age eleven, Ben had no behavioral problems at all. His Ritalin kept his hyperactivity in check and allowed him to focus in school. At home he was compliant and cuddly. As puberty set in, however, his behavior changed dramatically. Although he never threw tantrums as a child, he began raging in adolescence. He became defiant and stubborn. He argued about everything, whereas before he argued about little. His black-and-white thinking became even more starkly defined. He began to isolate himself excessively, even within the family. He was content to spend hours in his room and would rage when he had to come out.

During this time Ben quit taking his medicine. We recognized that it was not as effective as it had once been in helping with his mood swings, hyperactivity, and lack of focus. His hyperactivity had begun to wane on its own, but his moods had begun to swing more dramatically from happy-go-lucky to anger to sadness. It did not occur to me then that Ben might have Asperger's and not ADHD as originally diagnosed. As I learned more about Asperger's syndrome, however, I began to think Ben's development more readily fit into the autistic spectrum.

Like Ben, Leah was diagnosed with ADHD in early elementary school. She, too, had black-and-white thinking, was highly proficient verbally, and was extremely hyperactive. Unlike Ben, however, Leah was tremendously oppositional. At home, she would rage at the slightest provocation. She tortured her sisters regularly and once even chased them with a butcher knife. She would find snakes in the yard and throw them at her mother.

In school, she would dance on the desks, talk back to teachers, and devise malicious pranks. Socially, she would isolate herself rather than seek friends. She rejected overtures from girls who sought her friendship, preferring instead to play with boys since she was physically coordinated. She, too, became prone to dramatic mood swings ranging from dark depression to raging mania.

In addition to her diagnosis of ADHD, Leah was also labeled a behavior problem. (She was diagnosed before ODD was specifically classified in the DSM.) She, too, was placed on Ritalin; however, the medicine did not affect her behavior. After a while, she quit taking the Ritalin and told her parents that she had. At age ten she started self-medicating with drugs and alcohol to ease the mood swings and the feelings of isolation from not fitting in with her peers. She became a social chameleon, changing to fit in with whatever group she was around. Although she did not understand the social rules governing interactions, Leah mimicked the behaviors and appearance of the groups. Sadly, this tendency, as well as the awareness that she could not fit in anywhere, led to an eating disorder in addition to alcohol and drug abuse. She could not sustain friendships because she did not understand why her friends expected her to return calls, to share feelings, or to make small talk. Consequently, Leah spent her childhood isolated from her family, her teachers, and her peers.

Many children exhibit these same symptoms to varying degrees. The Web site www.conductdisorders.com gives numerous examples of children like Christian, who are "very smart but can't calm down to listen or follow instructions and [are] aggressive without medication." Or there is Heather, another bright child who "is an extremely demanding, hyperactive, and inattentive child" who is "noncompliant and disruptive." Another young girl, Nicole, was very compliant and did well in school until age eleven, when she became oppositional and began isolating herself from her family and peers. Like Leah, Nicole started having depressive episodes, took up drinking and smoking, and became extremely noncompliant. Now her parents don't know where to turn and are at their wits' end.

Although they present very differently in terms of temperament and behavior, many of these children shared several characteristics common to Asperger's syndrome. Despite their high level of intelligence, they could not comprehend the rules governing joint or two-way communication.

Several began to exhibit symptoms of bipolar disorder during this time, and all became socially isolated from their peer groups because of their developmental problems.

AGES TWELVE THROUGH SEVENTEEN

This developmental stage is one of the saddest and most difficult when examining children who have Asperger's syndrome and ADHD. During this critical stage, these children move through adolescence into young adulthood without the social and communication abilities that their peers possess. Consequently, they grow more isolated even though they crave more social interactions. As children mature they naturally reach out to peers and turn away from their families. Sexuality, independence, special interests—all of these come to the forefront of a child's life during these developmental years. Adolescents strive to become independent from their parents, and they turn to their peer group for direction and validation.

However, if a child is rejected by the peer groups or must change like a chameleon to function within the social setting, then the child develops an unclear perception of himself or herself in relation to others. One type of child will perceive that he is socially undesirable and so fixates upon special interests or pursuits to compensate. Shaun, for example, turned to running as his shelter from peer rejection. However, his pursuit of the activity was far from normal; instead, it became an obsession. He could cite times of all world-class runners as well as the times of his competitors and his running mates. He would train well beyond regular training times. He would run when everyone else was socializing. In other words, he would isolate within his activity.

Another type of child will strive so aggressively to fit in that he adopts different identities and overestimates his popularity. Hence, this child is actually more at risk because he is blind to his own social deficits. My son Ben, who is very active in our church youth group and is well favored, blindly believes everyone likes him. He has two reasons for this: (a) because they are Christians (and in black-and-white thinking this means loving your neighbor), and (b) because he perceives that he is central to the youth group, which equates to popularity. Sadly, adolescents like Ben tend to become the victims of cruel teasing, gossip, and rejection. One young man, Steve, was tormented incessantly in school. The other students would hide his gym clothes, call him names, and cruelly imitate his awkward mannerisms. In response, Steve withdrew. These types of children usually become so angry as to rage at the world or so isolated and depressed as to harm themselves.

One particular tendency of adolescents with Asperger's syndrome and ADHD that also affects social popularity is poor hygiene. Personal grooming practices such as washing one's hair, bathing, and brushing one's teeth are important at this age, especially where social impressions are concerned. However, as one girl reports: "I never became interested in how I looked.... I did such a poor and fast job brushing my hair, one day I found that all underneath it was one giant knot so bad, it had to be cut out with a razor blade."[1] Needless to say, when Asperger's syndrome and ADHD adolescents do not cleanse themselves regularly, they set the stage for a greater likelihood of peer rejection than if it were based solely upon their odd behavior alone.

As I mentioned in chapter 1, during this period of development when hyperactivity tapers off, bipolar characteristics tend to become more obvious. Mood swings become more dominant and extreme. Deeper depressions are more likely to occur during this stage, as are extreme rages. Destruction of self or destruction of objects also becomes more likely. Unprotected sex, alcohol, drugs, reckless driving, cutting school, defying rules, breaking laws—all of these are behaviors to which these children are prone. Shaun reports that his manias often coincided with his drinking binges and rages, which were then followed by depressive episodes. Once Shaun even tried to commit suicide by taking an overdose of his mother's tranquilizers. After years of enduring ridicule, of being misunderstood by family members, friends, physicians, and educators, these adolescents often seek relief in whatever form they can find.

Although autistic spectrum disorders and ADHD share the same sets of symptoms, not all symptoms appear at the same time or at the same degree of severity, which again makes diagnosis difficult. Likewise, not all individuals will exhibit all of the symptoms, again propagating misdiagnosis and mistakes in treatment.

What is also clear from these examples, though, is the pain, loneliness, and misunderstanding that these children feel. They have great difficulty understanding communication and thereby have a tremendous obstacle to overcome in socializing. And as if these difficulties alone were not enough, these children are often misunderstood by the very adults seeking to help them—their parents, doctors, and teachers. Consequently, as the faces of these disorders change between one developmental stage and the next, what begins on the part of parents as an earnest quest for help for their children often ends in despair, conflict, and even tragedy.

The answers are there; they're simply hidden in misdiagnosis and misunderstanding. With early and proper diagnosis, parents can understand and appreciate their child as he moves from stage to stage into adulthood.

Chapter 6

Careers and Relationships

Adults with ADHD and Asperger's Syndrome

If I have the gift of prophecy and can fathom all mysteries and all knowledge, and if I have a faith that can move mountains, but have not love, I am nothing.

1 CORINTHIANS 13:2

Most of you are reading this book in the hope of discovering answers to help your children. But what about your spouse, or even you? Do you find yourself trapped in repetitive patterns of behavior, regardless of circumstance, that are destructive to your relationships or careers?

Unfortunately, as with children, both ADHD and Asperger's syndrome cause tremendous pain and suffering in adults who are misdiagnosed or never diagnosed at all. Imagine the numbers of adults who have grown up without the benefits of medications and treatment. Teens at the mercy of mood swings, anxiety disorders, and oppositional behavior turn into adults whose struggles to maintain a sense of normalcy in their daily routines don't go away. Adults, too, self-medicate with drugs or alcohol, develop addictions to gambling, suffer from eating disorders, or simply find life too painful and commit suicide. Regardless of whether you agree with our premise about ADHD and the autistic spectrum, one thing is certain: These conditions are inseparable from the devastation they cause. They ruin careers, destroy families, and wreak havoc upon the patient and those around him.

As we showed you in chapter 3, both ADHD and Asperger's syndrome are first and foremost social-communication disorders. They are manifested in difficulties with reading social cues, attending to the give-and-take of conversation, interpreting facial expressions, comprehending multiple levels of language, and empathizing with the concerns and needs of another. According to R. Peter Hobson, people with autism "do not fully understand what it means for people to share and co-ordinate their experiences."[1] In other words, while they may appear to understand how to function in a social situation, adults with autistic spectrum disorders as well as ADHD do not seem to comprehend why people share feelings and thoughts. As psychologist Dr. Tony Attwood explains: "Although their social interactions with others appear superficially natural, they consider they are mechanical and not intuitive. They remain confused as to how others share intimacy and maintain friendships with so little thought."[2] While they may be capable of interacting (and do so at a very conscious level), the underlying ways in which people build and maintain relationships elude those with autistic spectrum disorders and ADHD.

RELATIONSHIP ISSUES IN ADULTHOOD

The intricacies, the subtleties, the interactions, and the emotions of relationships pose complications for these adults—almost on a moment-by-moment basis. The central difficulty for most adults with these disorders is the expectations of others. Other people expect these adults to behave, interact, and respond in ways that are "normal" or at least socially acceptable. For example, they will be emotionally engaged, able to empathize, capable as parents. Such expectations rule relationships among adults, especially relationships between friends, coworkers, husbands and wives, parents and children. And when these expectations aren't fulfilled, the relationships are seriously affected, as is the quality of life for the people involved.

Contrary to the stereotype of the loner who is content by himself, many adults with ADHD and Asperger's syndrome deeply desire friendships. They are acutely aware that friendships are a necessary and desirable part of normal life. Yet this awareness does not compensate for their difficulties in establishing and maintaining friendships—especially since friendships are based upon unwritten rules for interaction.

Part of the problem that adults with these disorders have in establishing friendships is that often their odd mannerisms and awkward, stilted ways of initiating conversation leave people with a negative impression. Even if they're successful in beginning a conversation, adults with these disorders tend to center their talk upon an area of interest, such as sports, and carry on to the point of boring their listener. Or, in other cases, these adults rapidly shift from one topic to another and leave their listeners in the dust, so to speak. In either case, if the adult who has ADHD or Asperger's cannot navigate the first hurdle to friendship (i.e., establishing a common ground through conversation), then he will not be successful at making friends.

If a friendship is begun, then problems often emerge that interfere with maintenance. The main difficulty for adults with these disorders arises from the expectations that friends have of one another. Friends expect phone calls. Friends expect to share time together. Friends expect to share feelings. However, these expectations exhaust the ADHD or Asperger's adult, often to the point that they abandon the relationship. One young woman with Asperger's syndrome wrote what essentially amounts to a "Dear John" letter to her only girlfriend. It reads:

> Dear Jenna,
>
> You've been a good friend and we've had some good times but I can't do this anymore. The phone calls, the girl talks, the feelings thing—it's too much for me. Your expectations exhaust me. I have to do things your way and I don't know what your way is. Don't call me ever again.
>
> Have a great life.
>
> Leah

Clearly this letter illustrates how difficult and frustrating friendships can be for adults with these disorders. Nonverbal communication, sharing feelings, and reciprocating social graces confuse these adults because they cannot empathize with others' needs. As a result, they may be able to meet their friend's expectations for a time, but ultimately the burden becomes too great and they or the other person break off the friendship. What often remains is a pervasive sense of isolation and of being inherently flawed.

This Is More Work Than You Know

When it comes to careers, people with ADHD and autistic spectrum disorders possess a creativity that is unmatched in the common worker. If a problem needs solving and it takes out-of-the-box thinking to solve it, you can be sure that the employee with ADHD or an autistic spectrum disorder will be among the first to come up with a solution.

If he or she is still employed, that is. Sadly, people with autistic spectrum disorders and ADHD share characteristics that make them incompatible with corporate America and many other employers for that matter. People with ADHD and Asperger's syndrome have been described as disorganized, talkative, gullible, clumsy, scattered, oppositional, and abrasive. These traits make it difficult for them to function in a normal work environment where they must interact with others and be able to multitask and organize schedules and duties. Consequently, people with Asperger's syndrome and ADHD either have difficulties finding and holding jobs or are self-employed in an area of specialized interest (very often with assistants to help them manage their days).

One math student, Eric, clearly had a gift for mathematics. However, he was dismissed from his master's program at Cornell because he could not get along with the undergraduate students he was tutoring. He enrolled in a community college and relied upon note takers to help him organize his classwork. Eventually he left school to work two jobs in the field of computers.[3] A story in the *New York Times Magazine* tells of a man named Phillip who studied acting at Harvard and was dismissed because he was rude to his fellow students. He was clueless, however, that his peers perceived him this way. "I had no idea that I was being rude," he said. "I thought I was actually being nice. But that's the story of my life: one long non-sequitur." He eventually obtained a diagnosis of Asperger's syndrome, which explained a lot of his difficulties in the past.[4]

People with ADHD and Asperger's have varying degrees of difficulty working with and for others. Office politics generally elude them.

Coworkers perceive them as abrupt (answering curtly and wearing an angry or bothered expression for no apparent reason) and prone to ignore conventions of reciprocal conversation, such as not making eye contact when talking, missing the subtle facial expressions and body language that convey meaning at a deeper level, and ignoring others' questions and the usual social chitchat. For these reasons, people with ADHD and Asperger's syndrome often struggle in the workplace. For them, making friends and political allies at work plays into their social difficulties. Because of this, work is not a place of security and comfort; instead, it is stressful and threatening.

Think about it. Knowing that others respond to them differently, having trouble empathizing with others, being a poor judge of whom to trust—all of these tendencies set the stage for frustration, anger, and alienation in people who have ADHD or Asperger's syndrome. Couple this frustration and alienation with their impulsive speech, and the stage is set for a fiery confrontation, especially when the employer or a coworker offers a bit of constructive criticism. Consequently, these people gain reputations as "hotheads" who are not team players. They may be phased out of their positions, fired, or they might succumb to the alienation and quit. My husband, Tom, once worked for a large broadcasting company and was their top salesman. However, he received the following evaluation during a sales training seminar: "Tom resists using emotion in his sales approach. He feels the emotional approach to selling is nothing more than idle chattering of uninformed salespeople.... He prefers his sales relationships be based on a nonemotional respect for each other. Tom may be too blunt and direct in answering objections. At times he may attack the buyer or attempt to show the buyer just how stupid the question was."

Tom's behavior was characterized in this evaluation as blunt, aloof, moody, overly intense, and withdrawn. Clearly, Tom embodies numerous characteristics of Asperger's syndrome: the social alienation, the abrupt approaches to others, and the lack of empathy. All of these affected his relationships with his coworkers, and he eventually left his position.

Another man whose job loss is closely related to his disorder is Gary. I met Gary at an ADHD conference where he was speaking and conducting workshops to support himself. During a conversation after a workshop, he explained that he used to be employed in a highly technical field but had been "phased out" of his position. The reasons sounded all too familiar to me: He was too blunt and direct with his managers and colleagues. He couldn't master the art of office politics because he didn't understand why they were important. In other words, Gary's social and communication deficits led to his demise in his career of choice.

THE MARRIED COUPLE, A.K.A. THE ODD COUPLE

ADHD and Asperger's syndrome adults tend to seek partners who can truly be their helpmates. They often marry partners who can help them manage their routines and handle their mood swings, as well as help protect them from the outside world. Dr. Attwood describes this tendency, saying that spouses who do not have Asperger's often serve as the family's executive secretary. They manage home, the children, and the finances as well as the limited social life that the couple shares.[5] Dr. John Ratey states in his paper "The Biology of ADD" that "often the [ADHD] adult has had very few intimate relationships because of an inability to form or maintain such relationships.... We have some clients who cannot bear to be physically close to another individual for an extended period of time without feeling trapped."[6] Obviously, this feeling would have considerable impact on any marriage. Other significant issues also affect these couples and, ultimately, the entire family.

Mood Swings in ADHD and Asperger's Syndrome Spouses

People with ADHD and Asperger's syndrome are notorious for having difficulties managing their emotions. In *Driven to Distraction,* Drs. Edward Hallowell and John Ratey list the suggested diagnostic criteria for ADD in adults, which include impatience, worry, mood swings, and mood instability.[7] These same emotional tendencies are present in people with Asperger's syndrome, who, according to Dr. Tony Attwood, have a high frequency of mood disorders.[8] As a result of these difficulties, oftentimes adults with ADHD and Asperger's syndrome will turn to alcohol or drugs to help stabilize both their moods and their responses to others.

Bipolar disorder is the primary mood disorder in ADHD and Asperger's syndrome. Remember that bipolar disorder occurs in at least one quarter of adults diagnosed with ADHD or Asperger's syndrome. The extreme mood swings, anxiety, and paranoia that characterize this disorder are enough to wreak havoc upon any marriage, as Rachel revealed when I interviewed her:

> One day I come home to a husband who is exuberant, energetic, and hopeful. Things are going well at work. He feels connected to others. He wants to be around the children and me. To him, the future is bright. Then he gets insomnia for several nights. Soon his exuberance morphs into paranoia. He thinks people at work are talking about him, even conspiring against him. Our children get on his nerves and he barks orders at them. He is abrupt and short.

> The future isn't so bright now—especially for me. The children and I walk on eggshells to keep from setting him off. I know that he's going to blow up; I just don't know when. And when it does come, I don't know if his rage will be directed at the boss, at me, or at one of our children. I simply pray moment by moment to say and do the right thing. Then…it happens…. Sometimes I'm verbally attacked; sometimes my children are. Sometimes my home is damaged. Sometimes I take the kids and leave. Sometimes I stay. Either way, I know that soon he will fall into that black ravine of depression and nothing I do or say will help.

When most people think of depression, they think of feeling "blue" or feeling down. However, to the bipolar person, depression is a physically and emotionally debilitating condition. According to recent interviews with two sufferers, Tina and Matthew, these depressions are painful. Their skin hurts. Their bodies hurt. Their heads hurt. Their souls hurt. No part of them is without pain. And sadly, while in these depressions, they are utterly without hope. Their one saving grace is that they know they will eventually cycle out of the depression. This is a saving grace for the non-ADHD or non-Asperger's spouse as well, because he or she knows that normalcy at home will be restored for a brief time. However, the whirlwind roller coaster rides of bipolar disorder eventually take their toll upon most marriages.

Another characteristic of ADHD and Asperger's syndrome adults is the tendency to sudden flareups and rages over trivial matters. Details like sloppy housekeeping or leaving the lights on can send these adults into a screaming rage. When our sons would leave the basement light on, Tom would fly into a rage and scream hurtful things about their not being smart enough to remember how to turn off a light. Once he even went so far as to remove the light bulb in the basement. Nearly immediately after he would say those hurtful things, he would forget what he had said—even though the boys' feelings would be hurt for hours. This propensity to use words to completely demoralize an opponent stems, once again, from the communication deficit and a perception of words as literal objects rather than vehicles for emotional connections. Consequently, it is hard for the ADHD and Asperger's syndrome adult to understand how feelings can remain hurt after the argument has ended. Needless to say, this causes tremendous heartache and alienation in the non-ADHD and non-Asperger's spouse and leads to many divorces.

Isolation and Loneliness

Another difficulty in marriages with ADHD and Asperger's syndrome spouses is the pervasive sense of loneliness and isolation. Frequent complaints from non-ADHD spouses include insensitivity to needs, immaturity, a lack of intimacy, selfishness, and a lack of consideration.[9] Likewise, non-Asperger's syndrome spouses also complain of insensitivity, immaturity, narcissism, and a lack of intimacy and consideration.[10] One woman, describing her Asperger's-syndrome husband, stated: "Living with him is like living alone."[11] The loneliness of living with an individual who is wrapped up in a special interest, distracted, and unable to empathize with one's emotional needs lets a spouse down. It is difficult to maintain intimacy, for example, with a partner who is prone to spend money without regard to the couple's current financial situation. Tom is obsessed with anything related to *Star Trek* and *Star Wars*. Once he bought the latest one of these movies even though we barely had enough money to keep food on the table. (Needless to say, his purchase led to fireworks in our home that night.)

Similarly, an ADHD or Asperger's syndrome spouse's inability to empathize or validate his partner's feelings frequently leads to serious arguments. Often, ADHD and Asperger's syndrome spouses cannot understand why their partners are upset about their apparent callous and inconsiderate behavior. Just recently, one wife told me about her anger toward her husband, who threw away some papers that were important to her. When she confronted him about his presumptuousness in deciding what was and was not important to her, he could not understand her anger. Instead, he approached the conflict by asking her to prove why they were important papers. She was angry, but he could not understand why; *he* didn't think the papers were important. He simply could not empathize with her need to make choices for herself. Others' feelings are regularly hurt by partners who always forget to do something asked of them or who don't remember details, dates, and events that are important to their spouse.

This inability to understand stems from what Dr. Ratey describes as "a lack of receptivity to, and a lack of reflective awareness about, the other's thoughts, feelings and behavior."[12] Essentially, what Dr. Ratey describes is the social-communication deficit that leads people with autistic spectrum disorders to misinterpret signals because of a neurologically based inability to comprehend two-way communications. (For a more complete discussion of communication deficits, see chapter 3.) This deficit gives rise to the ADHD and Asperger's syndrome spouses' incapacity to comprehend their partners' needs for emotional intimacy, let alone reflect upon these needs. Imagine the sense of isolation that non-Asperger's and non-ADHD spouses experience when they finally understand that their partners do not appreciate that they have special needs, desires, and goals. Such realizations can quickly fuel the end of the marriage. It also sets the stage for some intense feelings of alienation, inadequacy, and rejection. Consider these excerpts from *Letters, Thoughts and Poems Written by Family Members* posted on the Families of Adults Afflicted with Asperger's Syndrome (FAAAS) Web site:

> The feelings of rejection and loneliness play a major role in the lives of the Asperger's family. You and your feelings are not recognized or understood by the afflicted person. You keep giving and giving and trying to change your behavior and ideas and ideals, your hopes and dreams to "make peace," to please someone who doesn't need or want your emotions, your thoughts or your feelings. They do not comprehend what you are trying so desperately to convey.... Their inability to respond to you emotionally robs you of your self-esteem, friends, family, confidence in yourself.... It steals a "normal life" away from "normal people." (Anonymous, 1997)

This next excerpt is from a woman whose husband finally received an Asperger's syndrome diagnosis at the age of seventy-two:

> I have documented years and years of his decline, both mentally and physically. The only advice I was given was to walk out on him, get a divorce, and start living a normal and happy life.... For years I felt I was a victim.... I have written volumes about our "loveless" marriage. (K.R., 1997)

Remember Gary, whom I met at the ADHD conference? His disorder led his wife to divorce him because he was not meeting her needs. In addition to losing his wife and helpmate, Gary also lost his home and—even more tragic—his children.

Children from ADHD and Asperger's-Syndrome Homes

As parents, we all want to leave our children a legacy of hope. But what do they inherit as a result of being reared in a home with these disorders? One inheritance is, of course, the genetic predisposition to the disorders. As we said in chapter 4, both ADHD and Asperger's syndrome are inherited—children who have a parent with an autistic spectrum disorder have at least an 80 percent chance of inheriting the disorder.

Consider this: Most of the children being diagnosed now are being raised by a parent who was not diagnosed or who was misdiagnosed as a child. Consequently, the behaviors and emotional responses these children experience from the ADHD or Asperger's syndrome parent are nearly pure in their level of expression—that is to say, the children of today are being raised by parents who have not had the benefit of autism or ADHD awareness, intervention, or treatment. Therefore, these children are experiencing full force the ramifications of being raised by a parent with these disorders.

What are the consequences for the children? First is the issue of emotional isolation and alienation. One mother wrote to me of her husband's failure "to see how his isolation has the effect of isolating his family. He doesn't feel their loneliness and their pain over how they have failed to touch him or be touched by him. Life seems to erode more and more each day." Obviously, when a child fails in repeated attempts to connect with and affect a parent on an emotional level, the child begins to feel inherently flawed. Or worse, when a child seems to affect a parent only by making him angry, then the damage is even more devastating to the child's sense of self. A child may begin to behave in destructive ways to gain the attention he so desperately needs from the Asperger's or ADHD parent. Drugs, alcohol, sex, and even running away are common behaviors in children from these homes. For instance, one man told me he left home at age fourteen because his father was so angry all the time: "He expected me to be perfect, but I couldn't be." The young man never returned home but went on to become a minister.

My son Jeff ran away from home when he was seventeen. He jeopardized his graduation, his chances for college, and even his relationships with his friends and family for a girlfriend. Fortunately, we were able to get him back soon after he fled; however, his central motivation in his relationship with this girl was that she needed him. She made him feel worthy and important, like he had a purpose in life. Subsequent family counseling sessions revealed that Jeff's primary problem centered upon a troubled relationship with his father—the distance, the isolation, the anger, and the lack of communication.

We were fortunate with Jeff. He didn't turn to drugs or alcohol. But we did almost lose him to the effects of his father's autistic spectrum disorder. While we turned to conventional pastoral counseling to help mend our family during the crisis, such an approach would not help change the root problems and behaviors associated with the autistic spectrum. Unfortunately, counseling is typically the only remedy most couples and families seek in hopes of finding a cure that works.

FINDING HELP: WHAT WORKS

Traditional psychotherapy is fairly ineffective when dealing with changing the behaviors associated with ADHD and Asperger's syndrome that are hurtful to family members. The impulsivity, aloofness, abrupt responses, isolation, and emotional detachment that are markers of autistic spectrum disorders stem from biological and neurological causes; consequently, these are not learned responses—that is, behaviors that can be changed. The person with an autistic spectrum disorder does not deliberately act in a way to alienate his spouse and children. He does not plan to thwart his children's development by withholding affection. He does not intend to wound his spouse by ignoring her needs. He does not intentionally harm his family by behaving in certain ways.

Because the ADHD and Asperger's syndrome adult suffers from a social-communication deficit, conventional counseling methods alone do not work. Traditional approaches to counseling assume that the patient will be able to apply what is "learned" in the counseling session to daily interactions. This method also assumes that the patient is capable of analyzing the communication situation, assigning attention to competing stimuli, and operating within a social environment—all actions that are very difficult for the ADHD and Asperger's syndrome adult because all of these are tied to the executive function of the brain (see chapter 3 for more explanation of the executive function). Traditional counseling methods alone are oftentimes ineffectual when dealing with ADHD and Asperger's syndrome adults because of the biology behind these disorders.

Counseling is more effective when combined with proper diagnosis and medication. The catch, of course, is that a proper diagnosis is central to obtaining the right medication and the right information to help the family. The diagnosis affords the ADHD and Asperger's syndrome spouse and his partner the realization that he is different—not bad or mad or inherently wrong. I distinctly remember wondering why Tom would get so angry with me when we would take vacations. He would react to every little mishap as if I were responsible. We would be in a strange city, and he would rage at me because I didn't know how to reach our hotel. If something went wrong with the rental car agency, he blamed me. I took all of this quite personally. As I became aware of Asperger's syndrome and Tom received a diagnosis, however, it all clicked. He wasn't reacting to *me;* he was responding to massive changes in his routine. This knowledge has helped me better prepare for trips now. As a result, Tom's travels are less traumatic, and mine are far more peaceful.

By minimizing the mood disorders and the impulsivity through medication, traditional counseling methods have a greater chance of paving the way for increased awareness and understanding of each other. With proper medication mitigating the symptoms of ADHD and Asperger's syndrome, the patient can be led to "understand why other people do what they do, and how he or she can put this information to use in responding to difficult situations."[13] Improved dialog opens pathways for the couple to recognize the differences in how each thinks about and responds to the world, for them to learn strategies to manage their emotions, and for them to seek support from local groups, national organizations, and Internet groups. Ultimately, the goal is to promote true understanding, better communication, and a healthier family environment for ADHD and Asperger's syndrome adults.

Chapter 7 presents a more complete survey of other methods that have proven helpful in managing the symptoms of ADHD and Asperger's syndrome, but here's a brief overview: Coaching and social stories can help ADHD and Asperger's adults organize daily routines and manage social interactions. Some occupational therapy may be helpful with addressing sensory issues. As for mood and behavioral issues, a diet low in gluten and casein may help adults with irritability, bowel problems, aggressiveness, and inattentiveness, though studies are presently inconclusive on this issue. Exercise, however, has been proven time and again to aid ADHD and Asperger's syndrome patients. Likewise, chiropractic and massage therapy reduce anxiety and tension as well as increase one's ability to focus.

As I've said before, the most successful approach for these disorders is one that integrates several therapies rather than just one. And ultimately, for adults with these disorders, the importance of an accurate diagnosis, proper treatment, and increased levels of awareness can mean the difference between a lifetime of frustration and isolation.

Chapter 7

Treatments for ADHD and Autism

An Overview

Tell me and I'll forget; show me and I may remember;
involve me and I'll understand.

CHINESE PROVERB

As parents with a diagnosis, we eagerly pursue answers. But where we wind up is at the very same point where my writing partner, Becky, and I became more than partners: We became mothers determined to find the most effective treatment for our children. As she lamented the lack of real answers available in ADHD literature, I explained to her how autism afforded more solutions for her daughter, who had recently been diagnosed. It didn't take much for her to become convinced that ADHD and autism were related, since she had already scoured the ADHD and learning disabilities literature and found it full of behavioral modification approaches she had already tried. Likewise, most of you who have children lost in the Bermuda Triangle of ADHD diagnoses have found that truly successful treatments are nearly impossible to obtain.

Often, the initial diagnosis of ADHD brings relief, then stimulants, and then confusion; their children still exhibit extreme behaviors. Next come labels like ODD, CD, and perhaps bipolar disorder. Along with these come the antidepressants and mood stabilizers. When these bring only mild relief, many turn to counseling, occupational therapy, educational modifications, and special diets. Polly Yarnall, who has spent the last twenty years working with developmental disabilities and has served as vice president of the Autism Society of California, has this to say about the parents' search for effective treatment: "If one misperceives, one is quite likely to misrespond. And, in the case of [professionals] working with that person, should they misread his behavior (e.g., attributing the behavior to conscious intent—which *can* be modified—rather than to organicity—which *cannot* be modified), then the interventions may yield disappointing results."[1]

The most effective treatments are those that begin to address the developmental deficits before the behavior issues emerge. Otherwise, the treatments become focused upon the secondary manifestations of the underlying deficits rather than addressing the organic cause of the disorder.[2] Of course, as I pointed out in chapter 4, the real origins of these disorders have yet to be discovered, though autism research is certainly closer to its genetic underpinnings than ADHD research is. Until treatment can be based upon the organic nature of these disorders, then the best option we have is an early and accurate diagnosis. Of course, such a diagnosis would hinge upon parents and physicians being aware enough of autistic spectrum disorders to screen for these as routinely as ADHD, but at an earlier age. An early and proper diagnosis would also hinge upon physicians and researchers in autism finding ways to recognize signs of these developmental disorders in younger, preschool-age children. As it currently stands, however, once a child receives a diagnosis of an autistic spectrum disorder, immediate assistance is available and encouraged. Autism literature abounds with calls for early intervention and does an excellent job of educating the parent advocates concerning the services available to help them and their children.

Interestingly enough, the treatments for ADHD and autistic spectrum disorders are nearly identical—mainly because the disorders appear to be closely related in terms of their biological origins as well as their social, behavioral, cognitive, and physical symptoms. Both ADHD and autism offer what appears to be a hodgepodge of treatments pieced together to address the core symptoms. However, while the NIMH has criticized ADHD professionals for inconsistencies in treatment and follow-up, the field of autism strongly promotes an integrated treatment plan and routine follow-up of its patients. Both fields advocate the use of similar approaches, though the effectiveness of the therapies depends largely upon how early the interventions are begun and the severity of the deficits.

LANGUAGE THERAPY

As we established in chapter 3, language disorders are intrinsic to ADHD and autism. Consequently, the most effective language therapies focus primarily upon the communication issues that these patients face. There is, of course, basic speech remediation for children who have auditory processing deficits that affect the quality of their speech. The goal of this level of instruction is to teach the proper articulation of sounds and words as well as inflection, prosody, and tone.

Effective language therapy for children with ADHD and autism addresses the other communication issues these patients face. A good language therapist will work to alleviate the verbal and nonverbal communication deficits that affect the child's whole behavior rather than focus narrowly upon only one aspect, such as speech. Instead, helping the patient learn to initiate conversation, to listen, to take turns, and to be aware of nonverbal cues are the approaches that will benefit the ADHD and Asperger's syndrome child most significantly.

BEHAVIORAL-SOCIAL TREATMENTS AND APPROACHES

There are myriad interventions designed to improve ADHD and Asperger's patients' abilities to manage their behavior and social deficits. All of these approaches operate from the assumption that the patient can learn the desired behaviors and responses, but some are more effective than others. Behavioral management practices that rely upon rote learning have come under scrutiny in the field of autism because, as B. J. Freeman, Ph.D., a professor of medical psychology at UCLA, maintains, these practices assume that the child also learns the concepts beneath the behavior. Yet, for autistic children, this just isn't the case:

> If you teach a child to put a block in the box, and you use the same block and the same box every time, he will learn it—but all he's learned is to put that particular block into that particular box. If you change the block or change the box, he's lost. He hasn't learned the concept of "inside."[3]

In other words, this type of approach may indeed teach a behavior, but it does not teach the underlying concept of *why* the behavior is appropriate in a given situation. Instead of rote approaches, behavioral treatments that rely upon contextual and situational strategies and feedback are more effective for patients with autistic spectrum disorders. These types of approaches go further in teaching the concepts underlying the behavior, or in the case of some approaches, at least help the patient manage the behavior.

Applied Behavior Analysis (ABA)

Applied Behavior Analysis (ABA) is an approach that has been used in varying forms to treat autism. According to Lynn Hamilton in her book *Facing Autism,* ABA breaks a complex task into smaller ones that can be learned more easily. Each smaller task builds upon the previous one until the entire task is mastered. She says, "rewards...are given for correct responses or behaviors while inappropriate responses are corrected, ignored, or rejected. Precise data on each learning trial [for each task] is recorded, and adjustments in the educational program are made accordingly."[4] She explains that ABA addresses not only behaviors but such skill areas as attending, imitation, language, social, self-help, and academic.[5] These skill areas are necessary for daily functions such as sitting in a chair, paying attention, playing, talking, dressing, grooming, and learning. However, the overriding goals of ABA are to promote in the child a desire to learn and the idea that he or she can learn.[6]

Initially ABA approaches learning as a matter of mastering tasks and skills—an approach that is still fundamentally rote learning. However, as a child develops, ABA focuses on making the connection between the *underlying* reason, or the *why,* and the behavior as an important part of the lesson. ABA has been beneficial for many children on the autistic spectrum. According to Lynn Hamilton, "About 90 percent of those who use it improve dramatically."

Coaching

Coaching is one approach that helps children and adults learn to manage necessary behaviors and skills. The field of ADHD advocates the use of coaching as a way to help a patient learn to do the things needed to function on a daily basis. As you may recall from chapter 3, weak organizational skills, an inability to set priorities, and difficulties in breaking down tasks are all problems stemming from deficits in the executive function. Coaching uses a cognitive approach to social awareness and to its ways of controlling impulsive/hyperactive responses and behaviors. The premise behind coaching is that by working one-on-one with a coach, the patient and coach both become aware of the patient's weaknesses and how he or she functions. Then, using this awareness, a coach helps the patient by supplying regular occasions for supervised skills practice. A coach is someone to whom the patient is accountable. Thus, through scheduled meetings and even daily phone contact, the patient reports to the coach and receives constructive feedback about daily life skills.

It is important to note that a coach is not a psychotherapist. While the coach may be aware of some of the more personal issues in a patient's life, the coach's role is to assist the patient with developing the skills and abilities that will help him or her function more effectively in the daily routine. However, coaching is one behavioral therapy that relies upon both rote learning and contextual strategies to help patients manage behaviors and skills.

Social Stories

One method used primarily in the field of autism is social stories. These stories are intended to give the patient direct access to relevant social information. Social stories are intended to be used independently by the learner so that he does not have to filter the competing social information coming from the teacher. Consequently, the lessons of the stories are internalized more readily.

In addition to the social information, the stories specifically highlight the perspective of others as well as the expected behaviors. Often these stories are developed to help the patient deal with major social or behavioral issues and are sometimes used in conjunction with other approaches. And while this therapy relies primarily upon rote learning, it can promote subtle and simple changes in a short amount of time.

Floor Time

Dr. Stanley Greenspan, in his book *Playground Politics,* advocates the use of floor time to "help your child enrich and broaden whatever she wants to communicate." Dr. Greenspan describes floor time as a "special period—at least 30 minutes a day—that you set aside for...spontaneous, unstructured talk or play."[7] The important point about this time is that it is entirely child-directed—that is, the child decides upon the direction of the play or conversation, and you must engage actively. You are to follow rather than lead, engage rather than detach. What emerges from this interaction over time is a heightened sense of trust and acceptance as well as support for some very important developmental processes: "sharing attention, self regulation, two-way [or joint] communication, emotional ideas and emotional thinking."[8] Autism relies heavily upon this approach because it addresses so many of the core deficits associated with autistic spectrum disorders—namely verbal and nonverbal communication, attentiveness, impulsivity, and emotional separateness. (These very same deficits are found in ADHD as well, but floor time is not an intervention discussed in ADHD literature.)

An important point that must be made about floor time in relation to the other therapies discussed is that it does help children comprehend the *why* underlying the interactions. By having the child in charge of the interactions and the parent following, the child is not in a situation of being taught or having to imitate. Instead, as the child leads the interaction, he oftentimes discovers for himself the *why* or the underlying motivation for the behavior.

Parent Advocacy and Individual Counseling

So many books on ADHD and autistic spectrum disorders tell parents that the first thing we must do is educate ourselves about the disorder so we can help our children. This may seem redundant, but it is imperative that you seek out all of the support groups that you can to learn about your child's (or your) disorder. Parent advocacy is our first line of offense against the ignorance and misinformation surrounding these disorders. For more information about advocacy and support groups, see Appendix A.

Because the symptoms of ADHD and autistic spectrum disorders are biologically based, traditional psychotherapy does not significantly alter them. However, therapy that focuses on real-life issues and addresses goals and concrete strategies for attaining them can be very helpful in helping the patient cope with the disorder. Other ways that individual therapy can help are by offering an arena in which to discuss the struggles of living with these disorders and by promoting reflection upon the relationship between the actual disorder and its impact upon the patient's sense of self. However, we must note that it is imperative to find a therapist who thoroughly understands these disorders and their symptoms.

PHYSICAL APPROACHES AND THERAPIES

Numerous physical therapies are associated with the treatment of ADHD and autistic spectrum disorders. Some therapies focus upon diet, others on occupational therapy, and still others on exercise. It is important to understand that while all of these areas are integral to the treatment of these disorders, none offers a cure. The best we can hope for is a reduction in the symptoms that interfere with daily life.

DIET AND NUTRITION

Much has been written about the role of diet and food sensitivities in ADHD and autistic spectrum disorders. Much attention has been given to the roles of gluten and casein as causes of autistic and ADHD behaviors such as aggression, hyperactivity, and inattentiveness. Both gluten and casein are proteins found in everyday foods. For instance, gluten is in wheat, oats, rye, and barley; casein is found in dairy products. Research urging avoidance of these proteins is found in literature from both autism and ADHD, though the roles of these proteins has not been proven conclusively. Nevertheless, countless parents and researchers testify that diets omitting these products have given patients relief from physical and behavioral symptoms. Lynn Hamilton presents a very comprehensive discussion of diet in *Facing Autism*.

In addition to the gluten/casein connection, the Defeat Autism Now! (DAN!) protocol urges parents to pay close attention to the role of alternative treatments. In this case, "alternative treatments" refers to "using biological rather than pharmacological methods, that is, finding what the causes might be, and treating the patient accordingly rather than only using drugs to treat only the symptoms of autism."[9]

Deriving from the DAN! project initiated by Dr. Bernard Rimland and the Autism Research Institute, this protocol is the result of collaboration among scientists and physicians in the fields of psychiatry, neurology, allergy, biochemistry, immunology, genetics, and gastroenterology. The protocol was developed for physicians to use as a guide for effective assessment and treatment, and it addresses testing for gluten sensitivity and autoimmunity evaluations, among other things.[10]

Recent research in both autism and ADHD has focused on biochemical imbalances as contributing factors to some of the symptoms associated with these disorders. Current research has explored a possible connection between low levels of essential fatty acids and a host of gastrointestinal, language, and cognition problems. Supplements such as Omega 6 oils from fish and Omega 3 oils such as primrose oil and flax seed help replace the essential fatty acids missing in the body and thereby may offer relief from some of the symptoms associated with these disorders.

As more genetic, allergy, immunological, and biochemical research is conducted, more alternative treatments are sure to arise. For now, however, there are several resources available that discuss diet and its role in treatment. See Appendix A for more information.

OCCUPATIONAL THERAPY AND SENSORY INTEGRATION

Occupational therapy is extremely helpful in addressing the motor skills deficit common in both ADHD and autism. As parents, it is important to have your children evaluated for sensorimotor skills by a qualified professional so that both gross and fine motor development can be addressed. Occupational therapy provides important support in the areas of play, self-maintenance, and school or work activities. Although not all children with ADHD and autistic spectrum disorders suffer from motor skills impairment, occupational evaluation and therapy can detect specific areas of dysfunction and customize treatment to an individual's needs.

In addition to occupational therapy, one area that autism is greatly concerned with is sensory integration. So many of the difficulties that patients with autistic spectrum disorders experience stem directly from sensory overload; that is, the world becomes a painful and unpredictable place when one lacks the ability to modulate sensations. As Stanley Greenspan explains, "Some children are oversensitive or undersensitive to touch, sound, smell, or movement."[11] Consequently, they need assistance with learning to temper sensations.

Many approaches are used to accomplish this, including object manipulation, aromatherapy, art therapy, and touch therapy. For instance, Temple Grandin's squeeze machine applies pressure along each side of a person's body to help him with sensations of touch. Likewise, music therapy has gained a lot of attention recently as an effective way of addressing sensory integration. Through music, therapists can promote self-awareness by momentarily transforming the child's "habitual response into a communicative one" by interrupting ritualistic or stereotyped behavior patterns.[12] Music therapy also works to integrate auditory, kinesthetic, visual, and tactile stimuli to help the therapist train a patient's sensory perception. In an overview of recent research, Dr. Greenspan notes in his book *The Child with Special Needs* that "simply playing classical music in the background has been reported to facilitate language development in children. Children appear to benefit from playing different drumbeats to music and exploring the piano keyboard, or xylophone, as well as from participating in rhythmic movements as long as they don't become part of a rote routine."[13] Consequently, music therapy could benefit both ADHD and Asperger's syndrome patients.

EXERCISE

Exercise is a necessary component of an effective treatment plan. Exercise promotes an overall sense of well-being while helping to improve coordination, motor skills, and one's ability to learn. As Dr. John Ratey explains in his book *A User's Guide to the Brain,* exercise that requires a "strong mental component," such as soccer or tennis, increases social abilities, cognition, and behavior. According to Dr. Ratey, "Evidence is mounting that each person's capacity to master new and remember old information is improved by biological changes [such as chemical alterations and neural organization] in the brain brought on by physical activity."[14] Rhythmic exercise, such as dance or aerobics, also improves the brain's ability to sequence activities and facilitates "the connection between intent...and motor planning," according to Dr. Greenspan.[15] Consequently, exercise is an important therapy for ADHD and Asperger's syndrome patients.

CHIROPRACTIC AND MASSAGE THERAPY

One effective approach to treating the symptoms of inattentiveness and hyperactivity in ADHD and Asperger's syndrome children is chiropractics. Chiropractic treatment can alleviate symptoms without the negative side effects that normally occur with medication. According to Dr. Warren Bruhl, a family practitioner, children with developmental delays often suffer from "a complex of physiological factors" known as vertebral subluxation—a condition that "can either increase or decrease the rate at which nerve messages travel from brain to body and back again. The result is that the child's brain cannot communicate with his body."[16] Significantly, vertebral subluxation is caused by trauma, emotions, and even toxins such as drugs, food additives, and pollutants. Sam once had an allergic reaction to some cough syrup and broke out in hives. To treat him, our pediatrician prescribed steroids, which caused an even worse reaction. Given our experience with standard approaches, I was willing to try any alternative treatment, so I took him to a chiropractor. Within an hour of his adjustment, Sam's symptoms began to subside, and within a week he was completely back to normal. Even now, I take him in for adjustments to help him with the attentional and behavioral problems stemming from his Asperger's syndrome.

Like chiropractics, massage therapy offers patients some relief from the symptoms of inattentiveness and hyperactivity. In fact, a recent study in *Adolescent* found that adolescents who were provided massage therapy fared better all around. The adolescents reported that they felt happier than before the study began, and the observers noted that they were less fidgety at the end of the study. Their teachers stated that the teens stayed more on task and gave them lower hyperactivity scores based on classroom behavior.[17] Thus chiropractic and massage therapies have been found to reduce the attentional deficits and hyperactivity in patients with ADHD and Asperger's.

EDUCATION

Federal law has mandated several educational provisions for children diagnosed with developmental disabilities. The Individuals with Disabilities Education Act (IDEA) provides for educational accommodations and early intervention for children with ADHD and autistic spectrum disorders. However, children with ADHD do not automatically qualify for assistance under IDEA since ADHD is not a separate disability category; instead, like children with other disabilities, they must meet certain conditions—namely, they must have a mental impairment that significantly limits a life activity such as learning. Depending upon the severity of their condition, they may or may not qualify for services under this provision. If they do, it will most likely be when "the ADD is a chronic or acute health problem that results in limited alertness, which adversely affects educational performance" under the "other health impaired" category of Part B of IDEA or under the "specific learning disability" or "seriously emotionally disturbed" categories when these conditions coexist with ADD.[18]

These laws require schools to make modifications for students with serious educational impairment, which can include but are not limited to:

- placing the student in a smaller, special education classroom
- mainstreaming the student into a regular classroom with the use of resource teachers to assist with instruction
- using assistive technologies such as computers, spell checkers, tape recorders, and calculators
- providing speech-language and occupational therapy

However, before a student can receive these modifications, school administrators and evaluators must develop an Individualized Education Program (IEP). This is a written statement of a specific educational plan developed for the child. It includes statements of the child's strengths and weaknesses as well as the instructional program designed for the child. IEP also includes the specific special education and related services to be provided, annual goals, short-term instructional objectives, criteria for evaluating performance, and the amount of time the child will spend in regular and special education programs. Parents have the legal right to be involved in developing and reviewing the IEP and should make every effort to be involved.

It's not as difficult to obtain educational assistance with a diagnosis of autism. If a child receives a diagnosis of an autistic spectrum disorder, including Asperger's syndrome, he automatically qualifies for assistance under IDEA. The same procedure applies regarding IEP, and the same services are offered. However, because awareness of the importance of early intervention has grown, the 1997 Reauthorization of IDEA extended the provision to include services for early intervention under Part C: Infants and Toddlers with Disabilities. The provision is intended to address the educational and developmental needs for children from birth to age three and offers these services to families with children who qualify:

- assistive technology: services and devices
- audiology
- family training, counseling, and home visits
- health services
- medical services
- nursing services
- nutrition services
- occupational therapy
- physical therapy
- psychological services
- service coordination
- social work services
- special instruction
- speech-language pathology
- transportation
- vision services

The aim for providing these services at an early age is to minimize the long-term effects of the child's disability or condition. And like an IEP, an Individualized Family Service Plan (IFSP) is created to guide and direct the administration of these services.

The aim of all of these provisions is to deliver the most effective treatment services at the earliest possible age. To this end, early and proper diagnosis is essential to building a customized treatment plan for each child and family.

MEDICATIONS

As I searched for answers to questions about medications for Sam, I met Dr. Paul Elliott at a CHADD conference. Dr. Elliott has a family practice in Dallas, Texas, and is a highly respected medical expert in the field of ADHD. As our friendship grew, I shared my discoveries about the overlap between ADHD and Asperger's syndrome with him. He, actually, is the impetus for this book. Over the years, he has urged me to publish my discoveries so that parents everywhere could help educate their family physicians about these disorders. And as a result of his encouragement and feedback, Dr. Elliott has become an important member of this project. Because of his expertise in the area of medications, it seems most appropriate for him to explain pharmacological therapy to you. Because of his unwavering support for this project, I've asked him to do so in his own voice.

Classically, medications were felt to be of little, if any, value in milder forms of autism. This was often simply an illogical extension of their not being useful in more severe cases of the autistic spectrum. In fact, when some medications were tried, they frequently seemed to exhibit a paradoxical response in the Asperger's patient—for example, marked overstimulation with the psychostimulants. Therefore, encouragement of further use of medications was abandoned early.

However, more recently it has been determined that a number of medications may give very significant benefit to the Asperger's patient. Both antidepressants and stimulants relieve many of the problematic symptoms associated with these disorders. However, it must be remembered that medications do not treat the core difficulties of these disorders; instead, they help relieve the anxiety, agitation, and obsessive-compulsive types of behavior and often moderate the patient's explosive tendencies, as well as ease depression and attentional difficulties. Dr. Fred Volkmar, a respected researcher in autism, echoes this view on the effectiveness of pharmacological intervention, saying, "Treatments developed are effective relative to certain disabling symptoms, but 'core' problems (e.g., in social relatedness and communication) appear less responsive to medications."[19]

Five types of medications that are regularly used in treatments of patients with Asperger's syndrome and ADHD symptoms are stimulants, anti-anxiety medicines, sleep medicines, hybrids, and antidepressants. (See Table 7.1 also.)

STIMULANTS

Beneficial Uses in ADHD and Asperger's

A number of scientific studies have now been published supporting the strong belief previously held by some physicians that aggressive use of the stimulants produced the best treatment of ADHD and Asperger's symptoms. A multicenter trial of children on methylphenidate alone, therapy alone, and methylphenidate and therapy combined showed that the methylphenidate-only group did the best of all the categories, *including* the group on both methylphenidate and therapy. The group on therapy alone did no better than children taking none of the treatments.[20]

One of the observations physicians may make when attempting to medicate the patient with Asperger's is that the stimulants, in particular, can produce a paradoxical reaction. In other words, the stimulant medications, instead of giving the patient more calmness and control of agitation, anxiety, and irritability, seem to exacerbate all of these features. Stimulant medications often provide a significant benefit if their dose is dramatically reduced. The customary dose for ADHD may need to be cut to one-tenth or one-quarter, as much medication as one is accustomed to using in treating ADHD. This may be rather awkward since dosage sizes often are not available in such small amounts. While one manifestation of Asperger's can be paradoxical—the patient reports that the stimulant stimulates him entirely too much, possibly leaving him unable to function—that same patient may have a much better and beneficial response to the same medication if it's administered in a much smaller dose. It is increasingly recognized that stimulants can help Asperger's patients with their ADHD symptoms. Consequently, Asperger's patients are reaping the benefits of appropriately smaller doses of the stimulants when they do experience the paradoxical reaction.

Usual Reactions

What should one expect as a usual response to taking one of these medications? Certainly, if we begin with too high a dose, or if we try to increase the dose too rapidly, the patient will likely experience stimulation. In some cases, this will be very uncomfortable, an unnecessary occurrence.

When using these medications, we can make no mistake by starting with too low a dose and moving up too slowly—other than patient frustration, of course. However, we can make mistakes by beginning with too high a dose or by moving up too rapidly. Therefore, we should begin with a much lower dose than we expect to be effective and increase by small increments every three to five days initially, and every five to seven days later. The purpose is to avoid overstimulation by giving the patient's body time to adapt to the stimulating effect of the medications so we may get the blood level up to the point where the brain performs the best. Handled in this way, the transition is very smooth, producing the best result for the patient.

Safety

Data collection will continue in earnest, looking for anything that might be a long-term consequence of the use of stimulant medications, but none of the things we feared twenty-five to thirty years ago might occur—such as permanent hypertension, heart attacks, strokes, growth retardation, loss of intellect, loss of memory—have materialized.

With the exception of Cylert (magnesium pemoline), which has been proven to cause liver damage, the stimulants in Classes II and III are among the safest medications we prescribe in the practice of medicine today.

Controlled Substances—Class II Stimulants

Class II Controlled Substances are the prescription medications that have the highest level of governmental control, oversight, and accountability. Several common brands are classified and discussed in this section.

Methylphenidate

Ritalin, RitalinSR. The Ritalin brand has been on the market for over thirty years and has been a very reliable product. However, it lasts no longer than four hours and often no longer than three. For that reason, RitalinSR was produced. It is advertised to last eight hours but frequently lasts no more than six hours with a benefit that may fluctuate throughout the day and vary from day to day. Therefore a substantial number of students have experienced a rebound effect in which their symptoms return (sometimes more severely), making physicians question whether the net effect is good or bad.

MetadateIR, MetadateSR, MetadateER. The Metadate brand contains the following forms: IR—immediate release (four-hour duration), SR—sustained release (six- to eight-hour release), and ER—extended release (twelve-hour release; a stable, reliable blood level for the duration).

Concerta 18, 36, and 54 mg. Concerta, which became available in August of 2000, is the newest of the products on the market. While it is methylphenidate, as are the other brands in this section, there are some significant differences that distinguish it from its competitors.

Concerta in all strengths is actually a plastic box shaped like a capsule. The coating contains an initially released dose of the methylphenidate to be dissolved in the stomach and absorbed quickly to release the benefit of the medication as soon as possible.

One end of the tablet contains a semipermeable membrane, which allows water into the tablet but keeps out other components of stomach and intestinal juices. The water is absorbed into a gel, causing it to expand. As the gel expands, it pushes up on the other component, methylphenidate4 in liquid form, pushing it out of a laser micro-hole in the other end of the tablet.

The liquid methylphenidate is in two bands: The first extruded is a weaker concentration of medication, and the last to be extruded is a stronger concentration. This is an important development since this design helps minimize the rebound effect many patients experience with other medications.

The sustained-release mechanism of the Concerta brand of methylphenidate is designed to control the rebound by starting with a weaker solution of the medication then extruding a stronger solution later in the day so the blood level of medication is greater in the afternoon and evening than in the morning.

Toward the end of the dose, at about twelve hours, the blood level of medication drops fairly rapidly until about the sixteenth hour, when it begins to taper more slowly for several hours, allowing patients to fall asleep fairly regularly.

Dextroamphetamine SO4

Dexedrine Spansules 5, 10, and 15 mg, and tablets 5 mg; The Dexedrine Spansules, the twelve-hour capsule form of dextroamphetamine sulfate, have tiny beads that are of sustained duration in the capsule. The different sizes of Dexedrine (5 mg, 10 mg, and 15 mg) all have the same type of beaded material, and the different strengths are obtained by the number of beads in the respective capsules.

Therefore, they may be disassembled, and a few of the beads can be removed at a time with an approximate count to get the Asperger's patient a smaller dose than those customarily packaged. While this is tedious, it may nevertheless be very effective.

Mixed Amphetamine Salts

Adderall tablets (previously Obetrol brand) 5, 7.5, 10, 15, 20, and 30 mg. Adderall XR, a twelve-hour sustained-release form, has been approved by the Food and Drug Administration (FDA) and will soon be available. Adderall has the advantage over Dexedrine in that it is not as likely to cause a persistent feeling of overstimulation, which patients often describe as "a pressured sensation," "agitation," or "edginess." It is a little less likely to suppress the appetite than Dexedrine but a little more likely to do so than methylphenidate. It is less likely to trigger the rebound effect than Dexedrine or the methylphenidate brand Ritalin but slightly more likely to do so than the Concerta brand of methylphenidate.

Methamphetamine

Desoxyn Tablets 5 mg—only remaining form; compounded in a twelve-hour sustained-release base. The main disadvantage to methamphetamine is its exorbitant cost. The Abbott Company, which currently has the only license to produce methamphetamine, has methodically raised the price of its line of methamphetamine products under the brand name Desoxyn to the point few people can afford it.

Class III

With the exception of Cylert, all the medications listed in the Class III Controlled Substance category were and are given for appetite control. As a group, the medications in the Class III Controlled Substance category don't work as well on average and have a poorer side-effect profile. That is to say that they have more problems with side effects for the benefits they offer.

Cylert's usefulness is probably at an end. Apparently most of the enthusiasm for it was because it was the only medication in the Class III Controlled Substance category approved by the FDA. The primary problem with Cylert, however, is its tendency to cause liver damage, sometimes severe, and in a few cases, life-threatening. While this reaction to Cylert is rare, the potential severity is very problematic.

The manufacturer recommends blood tests of liver function be performed every three months. This makes an already expensive medication even more expensive. As a rule, the early evidence of damage could be detected and the medication stopped. In most cases, the liver inflammation would return to normal, and the patients would do well. On rare occasions, early detection does not seem to help. Even though the medication is stopped, the liver damage can continue relentlessly destroying the patient's liver.

Most medications with a tendency to cause liver damage will have that effect in the first year of treatment. However, with Cylert, damage is just as likely to happen in the fourth or fifth year of treatment as in the first. The FDA required the manufacturer to warn that it is not to be used as a first line of treatment for anything but should be used with caution, if the case warrants the risks, when other medications have failed.

ANTI-ANXIETY MEDICATIONS

The medications for anxiety may be useful either on an occasional basis or for those patients who may have a chronic, residual level of anxiety or agitation related to a co-morbid mood or personality disorder.

Benzodiazepines

Xanax (alprazolam). This is a very effective anti-anxiety agent for relieving anxiety while causing very little drowsiness. Therefore, it is not valuable as a sleeping aid unless anxiety is the cause of the sleep disturbance. The approximate duration of action is six to eight hours.

Klonopin (clonazepam). It is a little more prone to cause drowsiness, therefore, it is also a good sleeping aid. The approximate duration of action is eight to twelve hours.

Ativan (lorazapam). It is a slightly shorter-acting medication than either Klonopin or Xanax and is prone to cause more problems with short-term memory, even in the oral form. The approximate duration of action is four to six hours.

SLEEPING MEDICATIONS

Sleep disturbances are more likely to occur in patients with Asperger's and ADHD, and they may persist after the symptoms are well controlled, though most nonpersistent difficulties with sleep are found in the first few weeks after medication is started. Two medications are very helpful.

Sonata 5 and 10 mg (zaleplon). Sonata is especially useful when the patient has trouble getting to sleep. A dose will produce sleep in about twenty to thirty minutes. One of its main benefits is that it lasts only about two to three hours. Therefore, it rarely leaves a patient with a "hungover" feeling the next morning. If the patient does awaken during the night but has at least three more hours before he or she needs to get up for the day, another dose can be taken.

Unlike most sleeping medications, Sonata does not usually make the patient feel drowsy as it begins its effect. Therefore, the patient must lie down with closed eyes, at which point sleep will ensue. If the patient waits to feel drowsy, he or she may be able to work past the period of Sonata's effectiveness.

Ambien 5 and 10 mg (zolpidem tartrate). Ambien is another very beneficial sleeping medication. It lasts about five to six hours and typically doesn't leave the patient with a "hungover" feeling the next morning. It does not have a tendency to build up in the patient's system, producing memory loss or a sense of drowsiness during the day.

"HYBRID" MEDICATIONS

This is a broad, unofficial category, which many physicians have described as "the hybrids." This term is used for several more recently developed medications because they seem to produce a variety of benefits that are outside the uses formally approved by the FDA. These medications were developed to treat other conditions but were found to have additional benefits. For instance, medications such as Neurontin, Carbatrol, and Depakote were released for the treatment of seizure disorders, though research has demonstrated additional uses beyond those that have been formally approved by the FDA.

One of the more recent medications often giving gratifying results when treating Asperger's and ADHD symptoms is Risperdal. Risperdal is available in 1 mg, 2 mg, and 3 mg strength tablets. In cases where Asperger's patients are being treated with Risperdal, the initial dose of .25 to .5 mg once, then twice, daily should be tried. This level will frequently be ineffective for adolescents and adults and can be increased more rapidly than would be done with an SSRI (selective serotonin reuptake inhibitor), until improvement in symptoms is obtained. This will allow for a patient's sensitivities, avoiding symptoms of too much medication. Beginning with a single daily dose at bedtime will allow the majority of any drowsiness that may be associated with the use of Risperdal to subside. Ultimately, it is frequently more beneficial to divide the dose into two times daily, but this will vary from patient to patient.

Risperdal and Zyprexa were initially approved as antipsychotics but have been more beneficial for such things as explosive personality patterns or a persevering oppositional behavior pattern that may bother the patient with Asperger's symptoms. Other medications such as Neurontin, Carbatrol, and Depakote were released for the treatment of seizure disorders, though research has demonstrated additional uses beyond those that have been formally approved by the FDA.

ANTIDEPRESSANTS

Many of the new medications may help much more than we previously anticipated. For example, the selective serotonin reuptake inhibitor (SSRI) antidepressants are well suited to reducing anxiety and tendency toward obsessive compulsive behavior that may be a feature in the Asperger's and ADHD patient, producing a significant amount of dysfunction in life. Starting with an SSRI antidepressant, we will frequently improve the patient's symptoms considerably. Though the SSRI antidepressants do not treat the core symptoms of these disorders, they do help anxiety, agitation, and obsessive-compulsive types of behavior, often moderating the patient's explosive tendencies and depression.

Furthermore, while these medications may have been approved for adult use down to age twelve—the standard cutoff separating children from adults for medication purposes—pediatricians frequently employ them in much younger patients. Generally, as research studies demonstrate their safety and effectiveness in pediatric patients, physicians use them accordingly, though formal approval by the FDA may be several years away in these cases.

Zoloft (sertraline). Zoloft appears to work the best to relieve the anxiety and OCD symptoms of the Asperger's or ADHD patient and has been used successfully to help these patients. Zoloft comes in 25 mg,

50 mg, and 100 mg tablets, each of which is scored for ease in dividing in half. For most purposes, the dose can be reduced by beginning with one-half of a 25-mg tablet (12.5 mg) and increased from this point, if necessary. With many patients exhibiting Asperger's features, the rate of increase may need to be slower than physicians are accustomed to. Beginning with 12.5 mg and increasing by an additional 12.5 mg at three- to four-week intervals may produce the desired effect, whereas more rapid increases may produce interfering side effects that are not being given a chance to abate as the patient adjusts to the medication.

While all of these medications function to some degree to minimize patients' agitation, anxiety, and explosive tendencies, it seems the Zoloft (sertraline) may be the best. The other antidepressants have not been as effective. And once again, as with stimulants, the dosages may need to be lowered to obtain the benefit without causing unnecessary side effects.

In this chapter we've surveyed some of the most effective treatments and therapies available to patients with ADHD and autistic spectrum disorders. It is important to note once again that a successful treatment plan will integrate several therapies instead of relying upon only one, since no single therapy or approach can address all of the symptoms and deficits of these disorders. Likewise, the best we can hope for from therapy is a minimization of the disorders' interference with daily life. At present, there is no cure for these disorders. Instead, according to a recent article in the *Journal of Clinical Child Psychology,* "not much is going to happen by way of improvement for all the disorders until the molecular genetics are unraveled and a top-down approach becomes possible."[21]

Table 7.1 Products and Substances Often Used to Treat ADHD and Asperger's Syndrome

Controlled Substances		
Class II	Class III	Class IV
Methylphenidate Ritalin, RitalinSR MetadateIR, MetadateSR, MetadateER Methylin Concerta 18 mg, 36 mg, and 54 mg *Dextroamphetamine SO4* Dexedrine Spansules 5, 10, and 15 mg, and tablets 5 mg DextroStat tablets 5 and 10 mg *Mixed Amphetamine Salts* Adderall tablets (previously Obetrol brand) 5, 7.5, 10, 15, 20, and 30 mg (12-hour form soon to be released) Biphetamine-T12.5 and 20 mg (in an ion-exchange resin for a 12-hour release)—equal parts of dextroamphetamine and amphetamine (rumored to be returned to production) *Methamphetamine* Desoxyn tablets 5 mg—only remaining form	Benzphetamine HCl (Didrex brand) 6-8 hour tablets, 25 and 50 mg Phentermine HCl Adipex-P 37.5 mg tabs Fastin 30 mg capsules—The brand is no longer available, though generic brands are. Ionomin 15 and 30 mg (in an ion-exchange resin) Melfiat capsules 105 mg (12-hour action) Tenuate tablets 25 mg (4-hour action); Dospan 75 mg (12-hour action) Cylert (pemoline)	*Anti-Anxiety* (alprazolam) Xanax (clonazepam) Klonopin (lorazapam) Ativan *Sleeping Medications* Sonata Ambien

Table 7.1 Products and Substances Often Used to Treat ADHD and Asperger's Syndrome (continued)

ANTIDEPRESSANTS		
SSRI's	Tricyclics	Other
(sertraline) Zoloft (fluoxitine) Prozac, Prozac Weekly, Sarafem, generics (paroxetine) Paxil (fluvoxamine) Luvox (citalopram) Celexa	(imipramine HCl) Tofranil (amitriptyline HCl) Elavil, Endep (protriptyline HCl) Vivactil (nortryptyline HCl) Pamelor (desipramine HCl) Norpramine (doxepin HCl) Sinequan	(bupropion) Wellbutrin, WellbutrinSR (venlafaxine) Effexor, EffexorXR (nefazodone) Serzone Tetracyclic—(mirtazapine) Remeron
"HYBRID" MEDICATIONS	NON-CONTROLLED SUBSTANCE MEDICATIONS (prescription required)	OVER-THE-COUNTER MEDICATIONS
(gabapentin) Neurontin (olanzapine) Zyprexa (valproic acid) Depakote (carbamazepine) Carbatrol, Tegretol (topiramate) Topamax (oxcarbazepine) Trileptil (quetiapine fumarate) Seroquel (ziprasidone) Geodone (modafinil) Provigil	(buspirone HCI) Buspar (guanfacine) Tenex (clonidine) Catapres	Decongestants Phenylephrine HCl (NeoSynephrine) Pseudophedrine HCl (Sudaphed) Ephedrine (MiniThins, etc.) Ma Huang (aka Ephedra) contains a mixture of ephedrine-like compounds Nasal decongestant sprays (Afrin, NeoSynephrine, Otravin, Dristan, etc.) Caffeine [Phenylpropanolamine HCl (brands—Dexatrim, Accutrim, others)—no longer available]

Chapter 8

Triumphs

Celebrating the Unique Contributions and Achievements of People with ADHD and Autistic Disorders

I do not feel obliged to believe that the same God
who has endowed us with sense, reason, and intellect
has intended for us to forgo them.

GALILEO

For all of the negative impressions that individuals with autistic spectrum disorder or ADHD foster (for example, their willfulness, rages, impulsivity, eccentricity, isolation, mania, and depression), these people are some of the most exceptional in our world. They are our visionaries, scientists, diplomats, inventors, chefs, artists, writers, and musicians. They are the truly original thinkers—the ones who, even in a corporate environment, think outside the box. They are the people so obsessed with their interests that they are the experts, the scientists, and the architects. In other words, these people are truly a driving force in our culture.

As the mother of a child who has Asperger's, I'm excited about the possibilities of the future for my son Sam. While I know the Lord creates each of us for a special purpose, I'm convinced that His purpose for people like Sam is as unique as they are. The blessing of originality of thought can extend from an individual to the entire world, provided the world can come to accept these people as an important part of the whole: "But in fact God has arranged the parts in the body, every one of them, just as he wanted them to be" (1 Corinthians 12:18). To this end, He gives all of us gifts that serve His purpose upon this earth: to glorify Him in all we do. And it is through the triumphs I'm about to share that we can see how these people have touched the lives of many by persevering in the face of difficulties brought on by their disorders.

I begin with my son Ben. Because of our awareness of autistic spectrum disorders and their associated symptoms, Ben's path has been different from the typical ADHD or Asperger's teen. Rather than being a social outcast because of his rigid adherence to rules and his childlike trust and honesty, these qualities have helped clear Ben's walk with the Lord. One area that has helped Ben flourish socially is his mission work through our church. This environment gives Ben the opportunity to share his testimony and work with others without having to endure their judgment. Consequently, he has been able to avoid the playground politics that so seriously hurt these teens. Instead, Ben has had the opportunity to travel around the world and work to bring others to Christ.

The next triumph I share is about my husband, Tom. Before we realized that he has Asperger's syndrome, our marriage was turbulent and stressful. This is not to say that with a diagnosis the problems go away; however, understanding goes a long way toward changing attitudes and hearts. Where I once felt bitterness and resentment, I now understood why Tom made the choices he did. And because he opted to go on medication, when we began marriage counseling with a therapist who was also aware of autistic spectrum disorders, our communication improved, and he gained insight into how his behaviors affected me and his children.

These insights helped him triumph in yet another way—in his relationship with our son Jeff. As I told you in chapter 6, Jeff once ran away with a girl, in part because he needed to feel important to someone. When he returned, he, Tom, and I began family therapy. In the process, Tom discovered that his relationship with Jeff was crucial to our son's well-being. Tom had thought that by providing for Jeff's physical needs he was fulfilling the role of a father, but Jeff had deeper relational needs. Through the course of our sessions, Tom came to a level of understanding that is indeed a triumph for a person who has Asperger's syndrome. Although Tom could not understand why Jeff needed this nurturing, to save our family Tom became willing to reach beyond his Asperger's tendencies and spend time with our son. They both began a martial arts class and have progressed through several levels together. More important, though, is the way Jeff and Tom have begun to relate to one another in ways I never dreamed possible.

Clearly, my family is full of triumphs over these disorders and their effects on others. But I want to report on two other people who were mentioned earlier—Matthew and Shannon.

Matthew is the man with the case of bipolar disorder. He's the one whose mood swings are sometimes so extreme that his depressions can be debilitating and his manias wreak havoc on those around him. He has sought pharmacological therapy to level out his mood swings. Finding the right combination and dosages of drugs has been a long and tedious process, but his life and his family's are being restored to normalcy. He has opened a successful restaurant that he operates according to Christian principles. Through this business he uses his tremendous culinary talents to lead and feed others.

Shannon, my close friend whose daughter was seen by Dr. Tanguay, has bipolar disorder and Asperger's herself. In spite of the challenges these disorders cause her to face, she is using her degree in social work to assist children with autistic spectrum disorders. She is naturally suited for this type of work—she understands firsthand the difficulties the children encounter. She has been a tremendous resource for me where Sam is concerned. But more important, she has become my best friend. Remember the difficulties that Asperger's syndrome adults have with making and keeping friends? Well, by finding a friend who understands these disorders, Shannon finally feels accepted for who she is. And by finding a friend with the honesty and creativity of Shannon, my life has been enriched beyond description.

Another triumph I must point out (although this is my first mention of him) is the executive director of Sam's school. He is an example of one who has triumphed over the deficits commonly associated with ADHD: inattention, impulsivity, and hyperactivity. He and his wife started this school, which is designed to meet the individual needs of each student. Under his guidance, the school's population has more than doubled in seven years, and new facilities have been added to accommodate its growing student body. One key to this man's success has been his willingness to adapt to his ADHD. Rather than trying to organize his days on his own, he relies upon assistants to manage his schedule and keep track of his appointments, meetings, and deadlines. As a result, this highly successful educator is free to influence the lives of hundreds of children each year rather than live frustrated by his ADHD.

Finally, there is Dr. Temple Grandin, the woman who wrote the foreword to this book. Her story is one of perseverance. Her mother sought out therapy and services even though conventional medical doctors repeatedly told her that her daughter was handicapped to the point of needing to be institutionalized. In part because of her mother's tenacity, Dr. Grandin has become one of the leading experts in animal-handling technologies. Her unique approach to thinking—she calls it "thinking in pictures," which is also the title of her best-selling book—allows her to design chutes and equipment from the perspective of animals rather than humans. Likewise, she developed something called the squeeze machine to help patients with autistic disorders find relief from anxiety and overstimulation. Most important, though, is her willingness to allow the outside world into her own. By speaking with candor about what it is like to be autistic, Dr. Grandin has pulled back the veil from a little-understood disorder and let in the light of understanding. Because of her tremendous determination and her ability to use her gifts to help others, whether man or beast, she has touched the lives of many.

Obviously, these examples are not what everyone would consider grand triumphs of a lifetime. Instead, we are conditioned by the world to view only outstanding achievements as triumphs. Yet within the everyday range of people diagnosed with an autistic spectrum disorder or ADHD, there are daily triumphs worth noting:

1. living in sobriety
2. maintaining a marriage and family
3. holding down jobs for extended periods of time

These victories, when measured by the standards of the world, are minimal at best. However, when viewed within the framework of the Lord's designs for our personal development, our roles within our families, and our contributions to society, these triumphs are hard-won victories indeed.

WELL-KNOWN PEOPLE HELD IN COMMON

As we speak of similarities between ADHD and Asperger's syndrome, it is interesting to note that both camps claim the same personalities as their examples of triumphs. ADHD researchers declare that Albert Einstein was a classic example of someone with ADHD. At the same time, however, autism researchers make the same assertion, suggesting that Einstein was autistic. Other personalities whom ADHD researchers claim for their own include Winston Churchill, Benjamin Franklin, Thomas Jefferson, and Thomas Edison. Again, autism researchers claim some of these same people as their own as well. Amazingly, both sides cite the same qualities as being noteworthy: disorganized, argumentative, brimming with ideas, socially awkward, inattentive, hyperactive, and not inclined to follow rules! It is these very qualities, however, that made them so important to humankind.

SOME INSIGHTS INTO THE BRAIN

It is impossible to discuss the contributions and triumphs of these individuals without understanding that their achievements stem from a singular ability to operate within the area of giftedness that the Lord provided them. That is, they use their brains in a way that is consistent with their uniqueness rather than merely trying to fit into the cultural norms. At the same time, we must see these people as part of the whole of our world, not just as gifted oddities.

I began to glimpse the importance of integrating rather than segregating people with these disorders while attending a seminar given by Travis R. Nay, M.Ed. Travis, a lecturer on several topics related to the brain, is certified by Herrmann International and the Pathways to

Greatness Program developed by Hal Williamson. I found that the contents of his seminar illuminated this issue of both uniqueness and how we might see individuals as an integral part of the whole. I have asked Travis to elaborate on his knowledge and understanding in this area. The following is his contribution.

Ned Herrmann, founder of Herrmann International, developed a four-quadrant brain model based on the physiology of the human brain. The foundation for his model is rooted in Dr. Roger Sperry's Nobel Prize–winning research of epileptic patients. Table 8.1[1] is a simplified version of the Herrmann Brain Dominance Model that represents the four quadrants of the brain and the characteristics associated with the corresponding quadrant.

We each have preferences for one or more quadrants. Our preference indicates the area of the brain in which we thrive. These preferences are our strengths and are generally reflective of our competencies. Table 8.2[2] reflects the diverse thinking preferences of many well-known people.

Unfortunately, most of us do not have a comprehensive understanding of the brain in general or insight into our own preferences. Individuals with ADHD or autism may have significant strengths in one or more quadrants. Identifying the way an individual prefers to think can help them and others around them appreciate, understand, and communicate with one another.

Failing to understand these preferences is particularly problematic within our institutions. Streamlined, efficient solutions are the order of the day. I would suggest, however, that manageable alternatives to "one size fits all" approaches can be achieved.

Table 8.1

WHOLE BRAIN MODEL

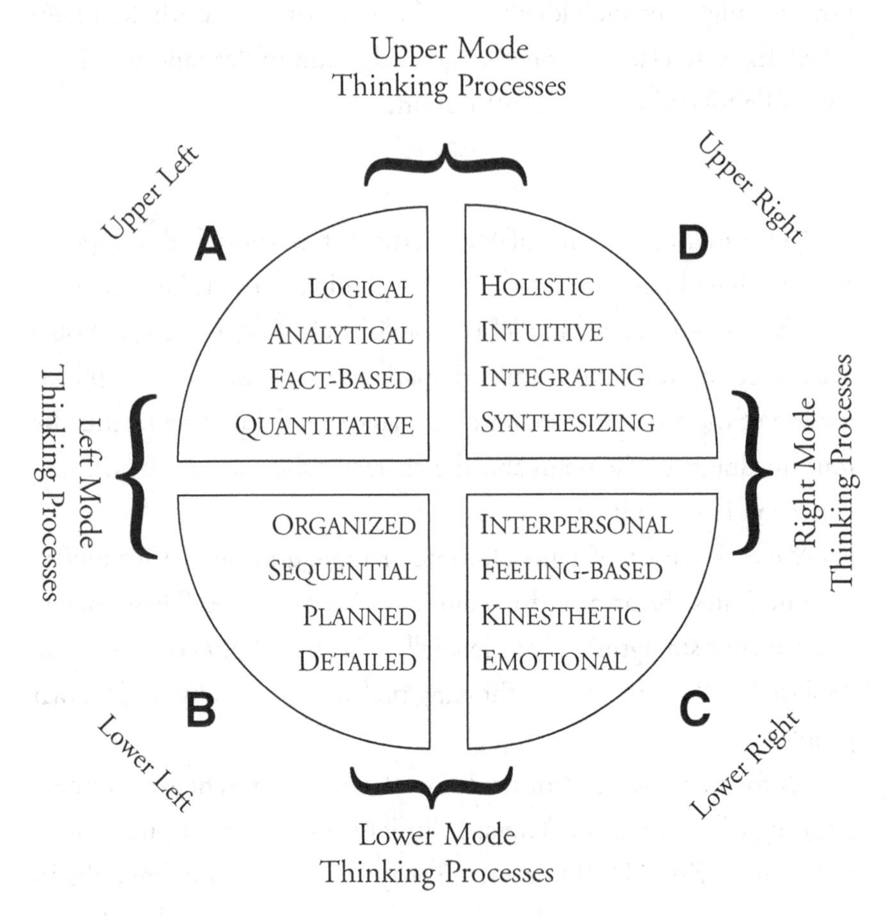

Table 8.2

HERRMANN BRAIN DOMINANCE PROFORMA PROFILE

The Diverse Mentality of Interesting and Famous People

A

D

Newton
Socrates
Galileo
Einstein
Descartes
Matthew (New Testament)
Chief Seattle
Madame Curie
Amelia Earhart
Irving Langmuir
Bertrand Russell
Hippocrates
Margaret Mead
Leonardo da Vinci
Adam Smith
Marilyn Vos Savant
G. B. Shaw
Picasso
Marco Polo
Spike Lee
Luke (New Testament)
Ben Franklin
Churchill
Malcolm X
J. S. Bach
Kant
Debussy
Thomas Jefferson
Jane Fonda
Aristotle
Mozart
Jim Henson
Plato
Phyllis Schlafly
Albert Schweitzer
Shakespeare
Margaret Thatcher
Betty Friedan
Eleanor Roosevelt
Gloria Steinem
J. Edgar Hoover
Jimmy Carter
Sammy Davis Jr.
Julia Child
Maya Angelou
Julius Caesar
J. P. Sousa
Chopin
Lao Tsu
Golda Meir
Otto Bismark
Mark (New Testament)
John (New Testament)
Louis Armstrong
Princess Diana
Samuel Pepys
Gandhi
Geronimo
Lech Walensa
Martin Luther King
Susan B. Anthony
Mother Teresa

B

C

Understanding our differences is the key to communication as well as to finding and learning our gifts. When people recognize and value one another's differences as strengths within a whole-brain context, no problem remains unsolvable. In the same way, if we can see past a diagnosis of autism or ADHD to the individual and his unique strengths, he will be freed to make significant contributions to the whole. The apostle Paul most clearly addressed this in Romans 12:4-8: "Just as each of us has one body with many members, and these members do not all have the same function, so in Christ we who are many form one body, and each member belongs to all the others. We have different gifts, according to the grace given us. If a man's gift is prophesying, let him use it in proportion to his faith. If it is serving, let him serve; if it is teaching, let him teach; if it is encouraging, let him encourage; if it is contributing to the needs of others, let him give generously; if it is leadership, let him govern diligently; if it is showing mercy, let him do it cheerfully."

It is clear from this passage that God created each of us to be a part of the whole, not to be complete in and of ourselves, but to have to rely upon others and their gifts in order to attain completion.

Nowhere is this concept of God's design more clearly illustrated than through the Gospels. By His choice of writers and the focus of each one's gospel, the Lord provides the perfect illustration of His divine scheme of the brain. An analysis of the backgrounds and writings of the gospel writers (Table 8.3) provides interesting insight into God's whole-brain design, which is used in this case to communicate the good news.

Consider how such a design might help each of us respond to God's purpose for us as individuals and as a whole. By recognizing, accepting, and embracing each person's uniqueness, especially the uniqueness of those who face the challenges of ADHD and autism, we can come a little closer to experiencing the ultimate triumph of living in His will.

Table 8.3

WHOLE BRAIN MODEL

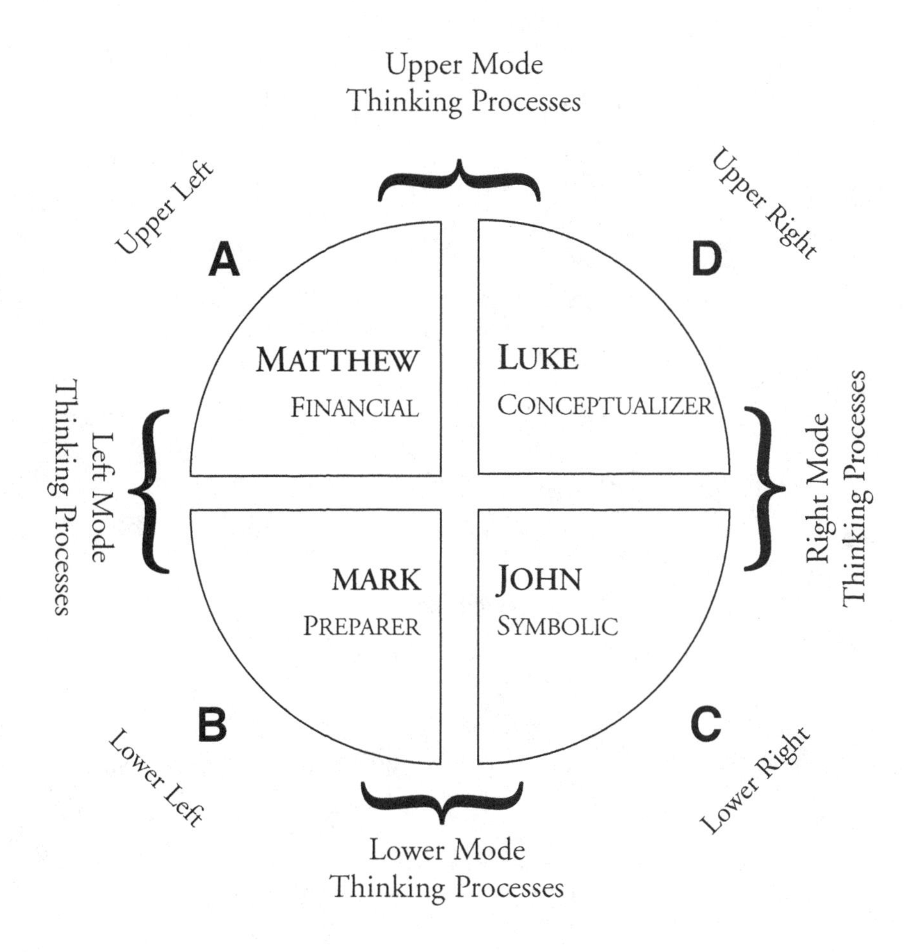

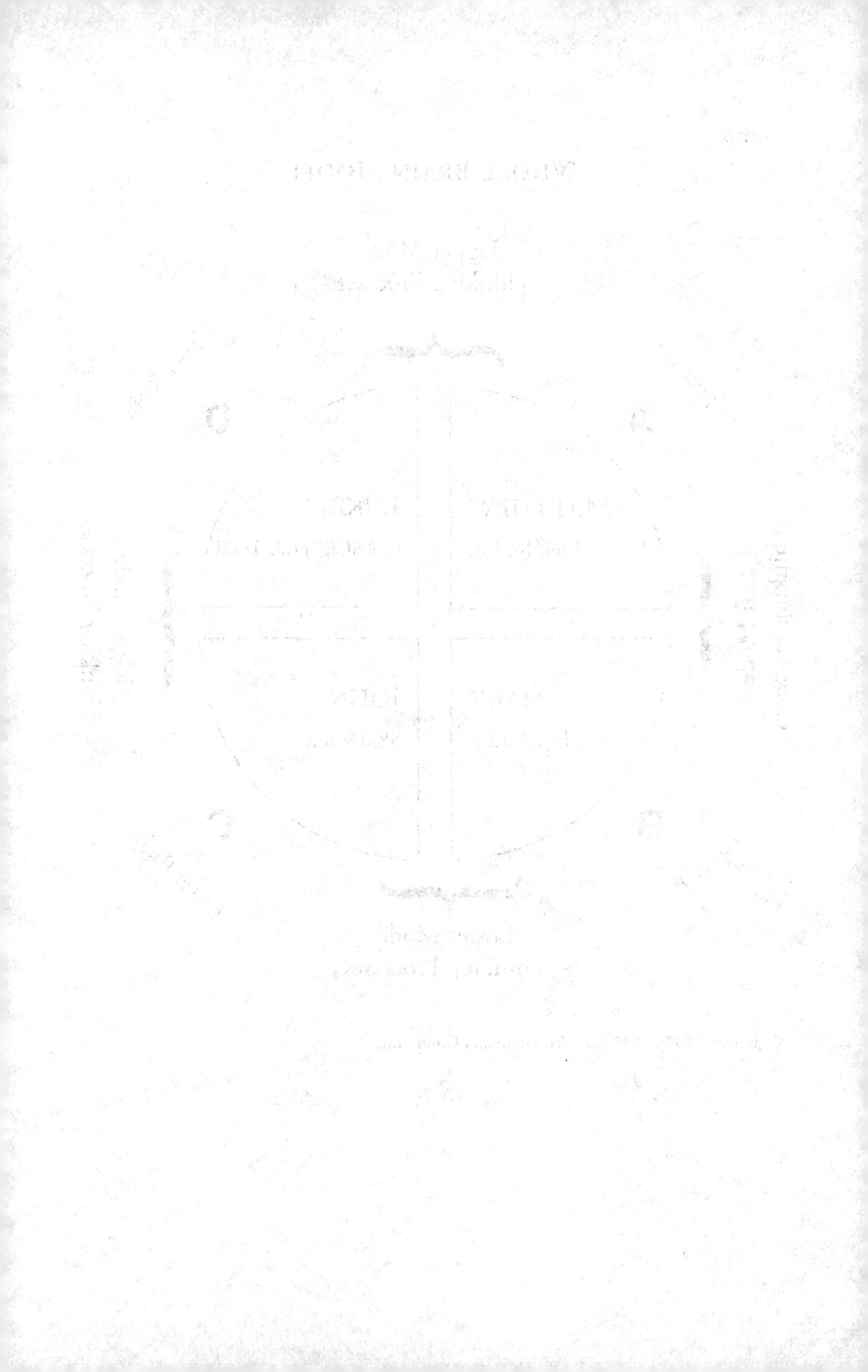

New Beginnings

Wisdom is the right use of knowledge. To know is not to be wise. Many men know a great deal, are all the greater fools for it.... But to know how to use knowledge is to have wisdom.

CHARLES HADDON SPURGEON

What began as a mission to obtain proper care for my sons has turned into a quest to promote earlier and better diagnosis, treatment, and understanding of individuals with autistic spectrum disorders and ADHD. To this end, I hope this book will encourage and facilitate conversations between caregivers and physicians, parents and educators, parents and other caregivers, and researchers in the ADHD and autism fields.

This last conversation is the one most necessary to the fulfillment of my quest, for it is out of such discussion that true progress can be made in the areas of diagnosis and treatment.

Yes, I anticipate battles within and between these fields. I expect some will dispute my claim that the disorders should be viewed as related rather than independent. On the eve of these most certain battles, I strongly urge researchers to avoid the usual debates about subtypes and instead begin by investigating the common origins, manifestations, diagnostic methods, and treatments for these disorders. I agree that subtyping serves a purpose by teasing out the various faces of these disorders. As the once-hot debate about Asperger's syndrome's relationship to autistic disorders clearly illustrates, however, researchers can err in focusing too sharply upon the search for differences; ultimately, too narrow an examination will harm the very people we seek to help. Dr. Lorna Wing addresses this issue, saying that even though a range of patients present with social, communication, and behavioral deficits, by applying the strict criteria for autism or Asperger's syndrome, "these subgroups make up under one half and considerably less if...the most strict criteria are rigidly applied."[1] I concur with this position and urge those professionals who can to turn their attention to helping parents and patients receive the diagnoses and treatments they desperately seek.

Current Media Trends

The growing need for shared research and discussion between the fields of ADHD and autism is reflected in stories that are beginning to appear more frequently in magazines, newspapers, and television shows. Story after story witnesses to the difficulties that parents face in obtaining an accurate diagnosis and finding appropriate treatment for their children. I related so intensely to one mother who wrote an article about her weariness that I began to cry as I read it. I recognized myself, my sons, and our struggles on that page. Such stories serve an important role in raising parents' awareness of these disorders and in validating their frustration and exhaustion. They are caught up, too often without warning, in the whirlwind of the disorders' developmental stages. As children move from one stage to the next and behavioral issues emerge and morph, parents' exposure to multiple diagnoses and multiple treatments is nothing short of mind-boggling.

The article that first helped me articulate my own struggle appeared in *Redbook* in 1996.[2] It affirmed my suspicions that perhaps Sam's difficulties were more than an extreme case of ADHD, which in fact they were. It also confirmed the difficulty so many parents face in obtaining an accurate diagnosis. The writer of the article searched for six years to find out what was wrong with her child. Experts gave her wide and varying answers: She was a poor parent; ADHD was the cause; her son was simply a brat. Finally, when her son was nine years old, someone put her onto the path that led her to Asperger's syndrome. Her son was subsequently diagnosed, and she began to have hope where she had only known abject despair.

As the number of ADHD diagnoses increase, and as public awareness of autistic spectrum disorders grows, related stories have become more common. Numerous articles about struggles with misdiagnoses of ADHD have appeared in newspapers across the nation: the *New York Times,* the *Washington Post,* the *Philadelphia Inquirer,* the *New York Times Magazine,* the *Knight Ridder/Tribune,* and the *Courier Journal. Newsweek* and *Time* magazines have featured stories about the difficulties of finally arriving at a diagnosis of Asperger's syndrome after beginning at ADHD.

The overwhelming responses to television shows featuring these disorders are by far the most compelling evidence of how frustrated and hopeless parents become when a diagnosis of ADHD does little to help them understand their child. On October 26, 2000, *Primetime Thursday*'s Jay Schadler reported a "devastating neurological disorder" known as Asperger's syndrome. *Oprah*'s "Explosive Children" episode elicited more than two thousand responses that indicated the frustration, isolation, and despair that parents experience when caught in a web of multiple diagnoses that stem from an initial diagnosis of ADHD.

I've met so many parents on my quest who see themselves in my story. I'm reminded of a letter that a mother sent me nearly seven years ago as I began my search for answers.

> Dear Diane,
>
> My six-year-old son has been diagnosed with PDD–NOS, but in my heart autism is a more accurate label. ADHD has been conveniently used by some professionals that have worked with us.... I notice the doctor writes ADHD on his Rx for Ritalin. Recently at a school meeting I slipped up and said that 'A' word and was flogged by three special educators in the room telling me not to use it: "Autism is such a negative word to most people," they said. I was highly offended, naturally. I felt like shouting "autism, autism, autism, autism."
>
> It's not a dirty word.

What this mother articulates is the complexity at the crux of misdiagnosis. Call it extreme ADHD. Call it PDD–NOS. Call it anything but an autistic spectrum disorder—the label simply carries too much stigma. This universal fear of autism works hand-in-hand with the rigid diagnostic standards that deny parents exactly what they need: the information to understand and help their child. They stand at the door of awareness only to be denied access because of the label someone gave their child. The field of autism is rich with answers that could help parents understand their child. But if the child does not bear the label of an autistic spectrum disorder, the parent is not granted permission to enter. On top of that, cultural pressure says: "You don't want that label. It's not socially acceptable." Sadly, this opinion on the part of the public arises from ignorance about autistic spectrum disorders and their similarities with ADHD.

Nowhere is this ignorance about the similarities better illustrated than in a pamphlet about ADHD that is distributed to parents in doctor's offices across the nation:

> For reasons we do not yet understand, some children, adolescents, and adults with LD and/or ADHD have difficulty recognizing social cues and using social skills. They miss the look on another person's face or the body language that suggests they are being annoying, and they blunder on. They may act inappropriately or seem immature and alienate others.[3]

Any parent or professional with an awareness of autism and its characteristics would see these as classic symptoms of autistic spectrum disorders. The lack of awareness about autism, however, in ADHD fields frequently misleads parents, taking them down the corridor of multiple diagnoses, improper treatment, and worst of all, total misunderstanding of their children and why they behave as they do.

Given the similarities in core deficits, the central impairments in communication, social awareness and behavior, co-morbid disorders, and the almost identical developmental patterns from age six years and on, it is *critical* that ADHD and autistic spectrum disorders be examined to see if they are indeed related. (Table 9.1 summarizes the similar features in these disorders.) By not doing so, researchers and evaluators will continue to unwittingly foster ignorance and bias against autistic spectrum disorders. This ignorance and bias are at the heart of NIMH's concern about the inconsistencies of treatment, diagnosis, and follow-up in ADHD; these inconsistencies are a major health problem.

It is my sincere hope that professionals from both sides will begin sharing information, evaluating each others' treatments and diagnostic options. With so much knowledge and so much dedication in both camps for the patients they serve, this kind of dialogue will pave the way for the research that will lead to solid answers. In response to this need, an interdisciplinary task force is developing, consisting of autism and ADHD researchers, educators, parents, and physicians.

Parent advocates and caregivers, you play the greatest role in promoting this awareness and dialogue—even to a greater extent than this book can. As you look deeper into the ADHD/ODD diagnosis in search of answers for your children, you can help educate the professionals. With more information about the ADHD/autism connection at your disposal, you can raise your physician's awareness of autistic spectrum disorders and, in the process, direct them to the information they need to more effectively diagnose and treat your children.

Most important, my hope is that all of you will persist in your efforts to find the right answers for your children at every stage of development. I hope you will not simply assume that the journey ends once your child receives an ADHD diagnosis. Instead, we want you to realize how closely autistic spectrum disorders and ADHD are related and how they manifest differently with age. In this way you can prepare yourselves for what will be the most challenging and rewarding effort of a lifetime: advocating for the earliest, most accurate intervention so you can help your child grow into a well-adjusted and content adult.

Table 9.1: Features Found in Both Autism & ADHD

- Inattention
- Hyperactivity
- Hyperfocus
- Impulsivity
- Behavior problems
- Social deficits
- Peer problems
- Language/communication
- 4-1 boy to girl ratio
- Impaired executive functions
- Genetics
- Treatment
- Uneven gross and fine motor skills or clumsiness
- Allergies
- Sensory problems
- Excessive talking
- Joint communication problems
- Temper tantrums
- Tactile/response hypersensitivity

Afterword

Before closing, I'd like to offer my collaborators an opportunity to express their feelings about this project and what it has meant to them personally.

After many years treating ADD and related disorders, I realized and became progressively more haunted by the fact that there seemed to be a group of patients who comfortably fit the criteria for the diagnosis of ADD but who did not respond very gratifyingly to treatment with medications. In fact, some actually became worse on medications that should have made them better. While such is seen with many disease processes, it seemed more pronounced and more prevalent when treating ADD than other diseases.

After learning of Asperger's syndrome, I realized this explained most of the cases of "ADD" that had been puzzling. I became even more convinced when I discovered that patients with Asperger's syndrome often react paradoxically to the stimulants, becoming very hyperactive and agitated. This set off my interest in pursuing the autistic spectrum, most particularly Asperger's syndrome.

I now recognize that those of us treating ADD too often miss Asperger's syndrome, especially when it is simultaneously present with ADD.

—Paul T. Elliott, M.D.

I need to state unequivocally at the onset that I am not a doctor. I am merely a father who, for the last ten years, has doggedly pursued answers and encouraged scientific research into the pathology of what we currently refer to as autism. My motivation for doing so is very personal. I have three children, two of them diagnosed as having autism. I need to be able to look them in the eye and tell them answers to their questions, whatever their questions may be. In lieu of that, at the very least, I need to be able to tell them that I looked everywhere. The almost total lack of information available when my oldest son was diagnosed spurred me onto a journey from which I will, most likely, never return. While I cannot personally undertake the onus of scientific research, I, like you, can surely play my role as a parent/advocate/participant in the equation. I can learn all that I can, help those whose efforts need championing, and collaborate with all those who seek honest answers to sincere questions. The latter role is my main reason for collaborating on this book.

Recently I was asked why I chose to become an active participant in genetic research. For me the answer was simple and similar to the infamous John Dillinger's response to the query "Why do you rob banks?" Namely, "Because that's where the money is!" Genetic research is "where the money is." It's the best vehicle that science has to ascertain the pathology, etiology, incidence, and onset of what we currently call autism. I say "currently" because I believe that our terms as well as our understanding are about to undergo a profound change.

I make no attempt here to appear authoritative. My goal rather is to share information that I have gathered in hopes of empowering families as well as further stimulating research and investigation into the identifiable etiologies of the disorders that affect our children and loved ones. It is my sincere desire to encourage you to join the research into what I consider one of life's greatest solvable mysteries.

—Carl Daisy

I am honored to have assisted in producing this book. What started as an exciting writing project became an incredible journey of discovery. As I listened, read, and wrote, I began to see with new eyes—eyes that the Lord opened through this work. I came to recognize my own daughter's and son's disorders and how to better help them. I also came to understand the nature of my husband's bipolar disorder and my role as his helpmate in the face of it.

I sincerely believe that God brought Diane and me together to fulfill a special purpose. I also believe that He ordained this project so that you, as an advocate, parent, or partner, and I, as a wife and mother, can minister more effectively to our loved ones. With all my heart, I encourage you in this mission and urge you to press on in search of the answers you seek.

—Rebecca S. Banks

Acknowledgments

No duty is more urgent than that of returning thanks.

SAINT AMBROSE

A friend once told me if you want to make God laugh, tell him your plans! She couldn't have been more right. When I first embarked on this journey, my intention was to educate myself about autism and related disorders to help my son Sam. Now, several years later, clearly God had other plans. Bigger plans. Much bigger.

I have come to appreciate the thank-you section of every book. Without a major support system, many books would never be written. This one is no exception. Dr. Peter Tanguay, thank you for your kindness, wisdom, and dedication.

Dr. Paul Elliott, it has been an honor and a privilege to work with you on such an important task. Thank you for having the insight and vision to suggest my notes should become a book to share with other parents and professionals. Your faith in me and support for this project have been above and beyond the call of duty. Your tireless devotion to this field and your patients is unsurpassed; you are truly one of a kind! Bless you and thank you from the bottom of my heart!

Through Paul, I met Dr. John Ratey and his wonderful wife, Nancy. John and Nancy, your energy level is the bright spot of any conference. I am blessed to know you both.

Temple Grandin, I am blessed to have met you and even more honored that you chose to write the foreword to this book. Countless parents and professionals have been helped by your efforts to understand autism and all its wonder. If ever there were an angel sent to represent the magnificence of autism, it is you. Bless you for sharing your life with all of us. Your mother's love has been an encouragement to me as a mother. I think I speak for mothers of autistic children everywhere: Bless you, Eustacia Cutler.

Carl Daisy, my dear friend, you have taught me more about autism than anyone, and for that I am eternally thankful. Your "nerdy" review on the manuscript was needed and will forever be appreciated. Your tireless efforts to help others search for answers is nothing short of angelic. Thank you for making me use my brain *(all of it!)*. I loved learning about DNA strands and alleles even though I complained a time or two. I am much wiser as a result. Bless you. Thank you for hanging in there with me while your own storms raged. You were, and are, an important member of the team. The love you have for your children is seen in all you do. This quote from Kahlil Gibran sums it up best: "For this I bless you most: You give much and know not that you give at all." You are a rare treasure indeed. I love you, my friend.

Joni Swift, thank you for being the first to point me in the right direction. Debbie Miller and Dee Hammond, "This message is for you!" Thanks for understanding why I couldn't call or write as often as sisters should. I love you both. Dr. Debbie Lusty, I miss our talks, and I pray God is watching over you. Thank you for your belief in this book. Kay Keegan, I am finally here! There are not enough words to express my gratitude for all the years you cheered me on to this goal. You're the best! God bless you! Richard and Vonnie Harris, the Lord placed you in our lives at just the right time and place. Karen Allenn Chitwood, thank you for continual prayer duty. Jim Galipeau, bless you for the wonderful friendship you have shown Tom.

Two who are no longer with us deserve a special mention. Helen Kennedy, for all that you taught me even though you didn't know it, thank you. Our family misses you. Kathy Price, your support during the rough years will forever be cherished. I miss you deeply, my friend.

Stayce Love, there is no question God's timing is perfect! Thank you for your input in the manuscript. Travis Nay, I see Christ in you consistently. You are wise and caring. My boys have been blessed by your instruction and touched by your spirit. As a mother I thank you from the bottom of my heart. Thank you for your prayers and support. I love you, brother. Kirstie, you are a gifted artist; thank you, bless you. John Isaacs, you are a wise and faithful brother in Christ. Liz Curtis Higgs, this section wouldn't be complete without a huge thank-you and a great big hug! Bless you for the late night e-mails, words of encouragement, and all your expert writing advice. You are an angel!

John and Teresa Savage, your friendship and loyalty through the years have blessed our entire family in countless ways. John, you care and it shows. Every student who has crossed your path is richer for it. Your belief in me during this project means more than I can put into words. You and Teresa *do* make a difference. Morgan Savage, you're an inspiration to know. Bless you, your brothers, and your sisters for all their help during this project. We love you all. Teresa Knittle, you have the patience of Job. Your endless support of this book has been a true godsend. Bless you for your wonderful friendship. I love you. Lynn Shannonhouse, I can't thank you enough for all the orange vanilla. Most of all, thank you for sharing as a mother. With your healing hands, there is no one as gifted. Bless you.

Heather Kemp, thank you for all your help. Your gifted ability to organize helped tremendously, especially your willing spirit to help in a flash whenever summoned. Bless you for being a cheerleader for this book; I pray it will continue to help all teachers better understand their students. Diane Twachtman-Cullen, because of your dedication and passion to help others, you have made a difference of global proportion in the autism field. Thank you for your wonderful insights regarding the formation of our task force. Communication is the key! You're an angel just like Lorna Wing.

Cindy Schwartz, you are a dear friend in the Lord. I know help is on the way, so hang in there. Thank you for always helping us look our best. We love you. My dear friend Chris Jolly, you are a wonderful mother, and your beautiful children are a result of that. Your keen insight and godly wisdom have been a blessing to this book and me. Your encouragement along the way has been "the wind beneath my wings." I love you, my friend.

Shannon Doyle Luedke, you are my best friend! Thank you for standing by me through rain or shine; that's what friends are for. To see a glimpse of the world through your eyes is to touch the stars. You are gifted beyond measure. Thank you for sharing your life with me and in the pages of this book. I know your patience has been tested; bless you for hanging on. You have kept me organized, on time, and motivated to do my best in the midst of your own storms. You're an amazing example of God's love. I treasure our friendship and am honored you trust me enough to be yourself.

Erin Healy, you are the reason this book will be able to reach so many people. None of it would have been possible without your belief and support in the first place. You are the "senior" angel on this project. I know why your kindness and sweet spirit shine in all you do: "Those who look to him are radiant" (Psalm 34:5). Thank you for patiently enduring every delay and trusting God's perfect timing. Erin, you're the best! Blessings always. Dan Rich, God bless you for having the insight to publish this book. Michele, Carol, and everyone at WaterBrook Press, thank you; you're all angels.

For my husband, Tom: Yes, you have done your jobs, all of them, very well. Thank you for all the times you disappeared without question when I needed the house quiet. Thank you for putting up with my crazy schedule, for taking over my jobs while I gave my all to this book. God made us a great team. Your faith in Christ has been the anchor of our family, and we all are held together by it as a result. For all the times you asked "when," we now have the answer: seven years to completion, God's perfect timing, and His grace to help us get there. I hope we can serve as an example to others. Interpersonal relationships can survive and thrive when love is the primary communication. I love you, Tommy. Bless you for being a wonderful father to our children and for believing in me and this book.

For my children, Jeff, Ben, and Sam: You all have grown up during this project, and it has become part of your lives, as you are all an important part of it. Thank you for loaning your mom out for so long. I am deeply touched you missed me so much, and I look forward to being Mom again. Jeff, your trials have only drawn you closer to God. Thank you for sharing them in this book. God knew what a born leader you were. It's your greatest gift. Carry on! Ben, your childlike faith is a gift from God; it is your armor. Keep it always. Thank you for sharing yourself with the readers of this book; they will be blessed, as I have been, to know you. Sam, why are you special? Because you're Sam, simple as that. It was you who led us to understand Jeremiah 29:11: God does have a plan for your life, and allowing you to be born was just the beginning. I can't wait for you to be in full bloom. I know your gifts and talents will touch the world as they have us. We love you, little buddy!

Rebecca Banks—yes, I saved the best for last. If not for you, this book would simply not have made it to the printed page. I know God brought us together as part of a perfect plan—mothers with a passion. I am so thankful He chose you as my helpmate in this project; I couldn't have done it without you. For all the 4 A.M. writing frenzies and the endless coffee supply, we still seemed to keep our wits. The real story behind this book is the tolerance of our families as they watched us from a distance. For all the nights you had to come here and drag your kids home at dawn, I thank you from the bottom of my heart for obediently following Captain's orders. Most of all I want you to know I tried to give this back to God a hundred times because I feared my inability to make sense of all this on paper. He had other plans, sending me not just any writer to help but a teacher of writing, the best of the best. Of course, when you ask, God sends only His very best. My friend, that would be you. Your writing gift is nothing short of God's music on paper; it is your language. This book will fulfill its purpose because you answered the call. I am so very blessed to call you friend. I love you, Becky. Thank you from the bottom of my heart!

Thank you, readers, for allowing me to share my discoveries. It's my prayer that you find answers here to help you.

I thank you, my dear sweet Lord, for trusting me with such an important mission and for sending me this scripture to remind me of my own gifts: "My heart is stirred by a noble theme as I recite my verses for the king; my tongue is the pen of a skillful writer" (Psalm 45:1).

Appendix A

ADHD and Autism Resources

Any of the following resources can be accessed at www.adhdautismconnection.com.

American Occupational Therapy Association, Inc.
P.O. Box 31220
Bethesda, MD 20824-1220
(800) 668-8255
www.aota.org

American Speech-Language-Hearing Association
10801 Rockville Pike
Rockville, MD 20852
(800) 638-TALK
www.asha.org

Asperger Syndrome Coalition of the United States, Inc. (ASC-US)
P.O. Box 351268
Jacksonville, FL 32235-1268
(866) 4-ASPRGR
www.asperger.org

Attention Deficit Information Network, Inc.
475 Hillside Ave.
Needham, MA 02194
(781) 455-9895
Fax (781) 444-5466
E-mail: adin@gis.net
www.addinfonetwork.com

Autism Research Institute and DAN Project
4182 Adams Ave.
San Diego, CA 92116
(619) 281-7165
Fax (619) 563-6840
www.autism.com/ari
www.autism.com

Autism Society of America (ASA)
7910 Woodmont Ave., Ste. 300
Bethesda, MD 20814-3067
(301) 657-0881
(800) 3AUTISM
Fax (301) 657-0896
www.autism-society.org

Children and Adults with ADHD (CHADD)
8181 Professional Pl., Ste. 201
Landover, MD 20785
(800) 233-4050
(301) 306-7070
Fax (301) 306-7090
www.chadd.org

Cure Autism Now (CAN)
5455 Wilshire Blvd., Ste. 715
Los Angeles, CA 90036
(323) 549-0500
(888) 8AUTISM
E-mail: info@cureautismnow.org
www.cureautismnow.org

Division TEACCH (Treatment and Education of Autism and Related Communication Handicapped Children, University of North Carolina at Chapel Hill)
www.unc.edu/depts/teacch

Families for Early Autism Treatment (FEAT)
P.O. Box 255722
Sacramento, CA 95865-5722
(916) 843-1536
www.feat.org

Families of Adults Afflicted with Asperger's Syndrome (FAAAS)
P.O. Box 514
Centerville, MA 02632
www.faaas.org

Future Horizons
721 W. Abram St.
Arlington, TX 76013
(800) 489-0727
(817) 277-2270
www.FutureHorizons-Autism.com

Geneva Centre for Autism (Toronto)
250 Davisville Ave., Ste. 200
Toronto, Ontario
Canada M4S 1H2
(416) 322-7877
Fax (416) 322-5894
E-mail: info@autism.net
www.autism.net

The Indiana Resource Center for Autism at Indiana University
Institute for the Study of Developmental Disabilities
2853 E. 10th St.
Bloomington, IN 47408-2696
(812) 855-9396

Interdisciplinary Council on Developmental & Learning Disorders (ICDL)
4938 Hampden Lane, Suite 800
Bethesda, MD 20814
(301) 656-2667
www.icdl.com

The Judevine Center for Autism
9455 Rott Rd.
St. Louis, MO 63127
(314) 849-4440
(314) 849-2721
www.judevine.org

Kentucky Autism Training Center (KATC)
Child Evaluation Center
Department of Pediatrics
University of Louisville
571 S. Floyd St., Ste. 100
Louisville, KY 40202-3828

Learning Disabilities Association (LDA)
4156 Library Rd.
Pittsburgh, PA 15234-1349
(412) 341-1515
Fax (412) 344-0224
www.ldanatl.org

MAAP Services, Inc.
P.O. Box 524
Crown Point, IN 46307-0524
(219) 662-1311
www.maapservices.org

National Alliance for Autism Research (NAAR)
99 Wall St., Research Park
Princeton, NJ 08540
(609) 430-9160
(888) 777-NAAR
Fax (609) 430-9163
E-mail: naar@naar.org
www.naar.org

National Association for Continuing Education (NACE)
10097 Cleary Blvd., PMB 510
Plantation, FL 33324
(954) 723-0057
Fax (954) 723-0353
www.naceonline.com

National Attention Deficit Disorder Association (ADDA)
1788 Second St., Ste. 200
Highland Park, IL 60035
(847) 432-ADDA
Fax (847) 432-5874
E-mail: mail@add.org
www.add.org

The National Autistic Society
276 Willesden Ln.
London, England NW2 5RB
0181 451-1114
Fax 0181 451-5865
www.oneworld.org/autism_uk

National Depressive and Manic-Depressive Association
730 N. Franklin St., Ste. 501
Chicago, IL 60610
(800) 826-3632
www.ndmda.org

National Information Center for Children and Youth with Disabilities (NICHCY)
Box 1492
Washington, DC 20013
(800) 695-0285
www.nichcy.org

National Institute of Child Health and Human Development
31 Center Dr., Bldg. 31, Room 2A32
Bethesda, MD 20892-2425
(301) 496-5133
Fax (301) 496-7101
www.nichd.nih.gov

National Institute of Mental Health
The National Institutes of Health
6100 Executive Blvd.,
Rm. 8184 MSC 9663
Bethesda, MD 20892
(301) 443-4513
Fax (301) 443-4279
www.nimh.nih.gov

Online Asperger Syndrome Information and Support (O.A.S.I.S.)
www.udel.edu/bkirby/asperger/

Pathway to Greatness and Thinking—Style Preferences
Seminars led by Travis Nay
www.HisImageMinistries.com
www.TravisNay.com

Sensory Resources
2200 E. Patrick Lane, Ste. 3A
Las Vegas, NV 89119
(888) 357-5867

Tourette Syndrome Association, Inc.
42-40 Bell Blvd.
Bayside, NY 11361-2820
(718) 224-2999
(718) 279-9596
www.tsa-usa.org

UCDAVIS
M.I.N.D. Institute
(Medical Investigation of Neuro-developmental Disorders)
2315 Stockton Blvd.
Sacramento, CA 95817
(916) 734-9040
www.mindinstitute.org

Unicorn Children's Foundation
5401 NW Broken Sound Blvd.
Boca Raton, FL 33487
(888) 782-8321
(561) 989-1140
www.saveachild.com

Yale Developmental Disabilities Clinic
230 S. Frontage Rd.
New Haven, CT 06520
(203) 737-4337
http://Info.med.Yale.edu/childstudy/autism

Zero to Three: National Center for Infants, Toddlers, and Families
2000 M St. NW, Ste. 200
Washington, DC 20036
(202) 638-1144
www.zerotothree.org

Appendix B

For Further Reading

Attwood, Tony. *Asperger's Syndrome.* London: Jessica Kingsley Publishers, 1998.

Autism Asperger's Digest (magazine). Arlington, Tex.: Future Horizons.

Patty Romanowski Bashe and Barbara L. Kirby, *The Oasis Guide to Asperger Syndrome* (New York: Crown Books, 2001).

Blakemore-Brown, Lisa. *Reweaving the Autistic Tapestry.* London: Jessica Kingsley Publishers, 2002.

Frith, Uta. *Autism and Asperger Syndrome.* Cambridge, Eng.: Cambridge University Press, 1991.

Grandin, Temple. *Thinking in Pictures.* New York: Doubleday, 1995.

Greenspan, Stanley I. *The Child with Special Needs.* Reading, Mass.: Addison-Wesley, 1998.

Greenspan, Stanley I. *Playground Politics.* Reading, Mass.: Addison-Wesley, 1993.

Hamilton, Lynn M. *Facing Autism.* Colorado Springs: WaterBrook, 2000.

Klin, Ami, Fred R. Volkmar, and Sara S. Sparrow. *Asperger Syndrome.* New York: Guilford Press, 2000.

Lewis, Lisa. *Special Diets for Special Kids.* Arlington, Tex.: Future Horizons, 1998.

Lewis, Lisa. *Special Diets for Special Kids, 2.* Arlington, Tex.: Future Horizons, 2001.

Myles, Brenda Smith, and Jack Southwick. *Asperger Syndrome and Difficult Moments.* Shawnee Mission, Kans.: Autism Asperger Publishing, 1999.

Ratey, John J. *A User's Guide to the Brain.* New York: Pantheon Books, 2001.

Twachtman-Cullen, Diane. *Trevor Trevor.* Cromwell, Conn.: Starfish Press, 1998.

Waltz, Mitzi. *Pervasive Developmental Disorders.* Sebastopol, Calif.: O'Reilly & Assoc., 1999.

Wetherby, Amy M., and Barry M. Prizant. *Autism Spectrum Disorders.* Baltimore: Paul H. Brookes Publishing, 2000.

Willey, Liane Holliday. *Pretending to Be Normal.* London: Jessica Kingsley Publishers, 1999.

Wing, Lorna. *The Autistic Spectrum.* Berkeley, Calif.: Ulysses Press, 2001.

Notes

Author's Note

1. Diane Twachtman-Cullen, quoted in Eric Schopler, Gary B. Mesibov, and Linda J. Kunce, eds., *Asperger Syndrome or High Functioning Autism?* (New York: Plenum Press, 1998), 223.

Chapter 1—A Mother's Mission

1. C. Church, S. Alisanski, and S. Amanullah, *The Social, Behavioural, and Academic Experiences of Children with Asperger Syndrome*. Found at http://www.tonyattwood.com/current.htm. 1 May 2001.
2. *What Other Disorders Have the Same Symptoms as Attention-Deficit Hyperactivity Disorder?* Found at http://my.webmd.com/printing/article/1680.50277. 28 April 2001.
3. Christopher Gillberg, *Screening and Diagnostic Classification* (McLean, Va.: The Interdisciplinary Council on Developmental & Learning Disorders, 1999), 20.

Chapter 2—Beginning with the Definitions

1. Bernard Rimland, *Autism Research Review International* 7, no. 2 (1993): 3.
2. Rimland, *Autism Research Review International*, 3.
3. American Psychiatric Association, *Diagnostic and Statistical Manual of Mental Disorders, Fourth Edition Text Revision* (Washington, D.C.: American Psychiatric Association, 2000), 69.
4. Center for Disease Control and Prevention, 1997.
5. Leo Kanner, "Autistic Disturbances of Affective Contact," *Nervous Child* 2 (1943): 217-50.

6. Hans Asperger, "Die 'Autistischen Psychopathen' im Kindesalter," *Archiv fur Psychiatrie und Nervenkrankheiten* 117 (1944): 76-136.
7. Maria Asperger Felder, quoted in Ami Klin, Fred R. Volkmar, and Sara S. Sparrow, eds., *Asperger Syndrome* (New York: Guilford Press, 2000), xi.
8. Uta Frith, *Autism and Asperger Syndrome* (Cambridge, Eng.: Cambridge University Press, 1991), 22.
9. Lorna Wing, *The Autistic Spectrum: A Guide for Parents and Professionals* (London: Constable and Company, 1997), 239.
10. Lorna Wing, "Asperger's Syndrome: A Clinical Account," *Psychological Medicine* 11, no. 1 (1981): 115-29.
11. American Psychiatric Association, *Diagnostic and Statistical Manual,* 84.
12. American Psychiatric Association, *Diagnostic and Statistical Manual,* 83-4.
13. Wing, *The Autistic Spectrum,* 58.
14. Wing, *The Autistic Spectrum,* 156.
15. Wing, *The Autistic Spectrum,* 156.
16. American Psychiatric Association, *Diagnostic and Statistical Manual,* 90.
17. American Psychiatric Association, *Diagnostic and Statistical Manual,* 85.
18. American Psychiatric Association, *Diagnostic and Statistical Manual,* 92-3.
19. American Psychiatric Association, *Diagnostic and Statistical Manual,* 93.
20. Frith, *Autism and Asperger Syndrome,* 6.
21. John Ratey and Catherine Johnson, *Shadow Syndromes* (New York: Bantam Books, 1998), 216.
22. Frith, *Autism and Asperger Syndrome,* 32.

Chapter 3—Which Is It: Autism or ADHD?

1. American Academy of Pediatrics, *Clinical Practice Guidelines: Diagnosis and Evaluation of the Child with ADHD.* Found at http://www.pediatrics.org. 27 October 2000.

2. Don Cohen and Fred R. Volkmar, *The Handbook of Autism and Pervasive Developmental Disorders* (New York: John Wiley & Sons, 1997), 296.
3. National Information Center for Children and Youth with Disabilities, Fact Sheet (Washington, D.C., 1998).
4. U.S. Department of Health and Human Services, "Surgeon General Releases a National Action Agenda on Children's Mental Health." Found at http://www.surgeongeneral.gov/library/mentalhealth/chapter3/sec4.html.
5. B. J. Freeman, "Guidelines for Evaluating Intervention Programs for Autistic Children," *Journal of Autistic and Developmental Disabilities* (1996): 5.
6. Compiled from *14 Point Checklist of Behavior Signs and Symptoms* (St. Louis, Mo.: Judevine Center for Autism, and *Autism* (Bethesda, Md.: Autism Society of America).
7. Compiled from American Psychiatric Association, *Diagnostic and Statistical Manual of Mental Disorders, Fourth Edition Text Revision* (Washington, D.C.: American Psychiatric Association, 2000), 85-92, and *ADHD Checklist for Children,* found at http://ADDultconsults.com. 17 July 1996.
8. American Academy of Neurology and the Child Neurology Society, "Practice Parameter: Screening and Diagnosis of Autism," *Neurology* 55 (2000): 473.
9. Tony Attwood, *Asperger's Syndrome: A Guide for Parents and Professionals* (Philadelphia: Jessica Kingsley, 1998), 103-11.
10. Christopher Gillberg, *Screening and Diagnostic Classification* (McLean, Va.: The Interdisciplinary Council on Developmental & Learning Disorders, 1999), 20.
11. American Psychiatric Association, *Diagnostic and Statistical Manual of Mental Disorders, Text Revision,* 4th ed. (Washington, D.C.: American Psychiatric Association, 2000), 93.
12. American Psychiatric Association, *Diagnostic and Statistical Manual,* 89.
13. Lisa Blakemore-Brown, "Weaving the Tapestry of ADD and Asperger Syndrome," *A World of Understanding: ADHD Issues & Answers* (New York: CHADD, 1998), 394.

14. Carl Sherman, "Core Features Identify Asperger's Syndrome," *Clinical Psychiatry News* 28, no. 2 (2000).
15. *Asperger Syndrome.* Writer's Corner, 2001, 5.
16. *Asperger Syndrome.* Writer's Corner, 5.
17. Temple Grandin, *My Experiences with Visual Thinking Sensory Problems and Communication Difficulties.* Found at http://www.autism.org/temple/visual.html.
18. Grandin, *My Experiences with Visual Thinking.*
19. Harvey Simon, M.D., *What Is Attention Deficit Disorder?* Found at CBS HealthWatch. http://www.cbshealthwatch.medscape.com. 1998.
20. Simon, *What Is Attention Deficit Disorder?*
21. Grandin, *My Experiences with Visual Thinking.*
22. Simon, *What Is Attention Deficit Disorder?*
23. C. Church, S. Alisanski, and S. Amanullah, *The Social, Behavioural, and Academic Experiences of Children with Asperger Syndrome.* Found at http://www.tonyattwood.com/current.htm. 1 May 2001.
24. Sherman, "Core Features Identify Asperger's Syndrome."
25. Ami Klin, Fred R. Volkmar, and Sara S. Sparrow, eds., *Asperger Syndrome* (New York: Guilford Press, 2000), 218-20.
26. American Psychiatric Association, *Diagnostic and Statistical Manual,* 81.
27. American Psychiatric Association, *Diagnostic and Statistical Manual,* 81.
28. American Academy of Pediatrics, *Clinical Practice Guidelines.*
29. Mark Wolraich, "Attention Deficit Hyperactivity Disorder: Current Diagnosis and Treatment," (American Academy of Pediatrics Annual Meeting, Chicago, 2000), 4.
30. Martin Korn, *ADHD and Comorbidity.* Found at http://www.medscape.com/medscape/cno/2001/APACME/Story.cfm?story_id=2262. 25 September 2001.
31. John Ratey, *A User's Guide to the Brain* (New York: Pantheon Books, 2001), and Russell Barkley, *ADHD and the Nature of Self-Control* (New York: Guilford Press, 1997).

32. Cohen and Volkmar, *Handbook of Autism.*

33. Barkley, *ADHD and the Nature of Self-Control.*

34. Diane Twachtman-Cullen, *The Invisible Curriculum: Where Essential Education Begins.* Found at http://www.autism99.org. 12 May 2000.

35. American Psychiatric Association, *Diagnostic and Statistical Manual,* 82.

36. Lorna Wing, *The Autistic Spectrum: A Guide for Parents and Professionals* (London: Constable and Company, 1997), 40.

37. Blakemore-Brown, "Weaving the Tapestry of ADD," 394.

38. Wing, *The Autistic Spectrum: A Guide for Parents and Professionals,* 157.

39. American Psychiatric Association, *Diagnostic and Statistical Manual,* 92.

40. Barkley, *ADHD and the Nature of Self-Control.*

41. Russell Barkley, *Taking Charge of ADHD* (New York: Guilford Press, 2000) and Ross W. Greene, *The Explosive Child* (New York: HarperCollins, 1998) and Arthur L. Robin, *ADHD in Adolescents* (New York: Guilford Press, 1998).

42. Edward M. Hallowell and John J. Ratey, *Driven to Distraction* (New York: Pantheon, 1994), 282.

43. Hallowell and Ratey, *Driven to Distraction,* 282.

44. Twachtman-Cullen, *The Invisible Curriculum.*

45. Twachtman-Cullen, *The Invisible Curriculum.*

46. Fred Volkmar, quoted in Jay Schadler, "Asperger's Syndrome," *ABC News PrimeTime Thursday,* 26 October 2000.

47. Lorna Wing, *The Autistic Spectrum: A Parent's Guide to Understanding and Helping Your Child* (Berkeley, Calif.: Ulysses Press, 2001), 37.

48. Wing, *The Autistic Spectrum: A Parent's Guide,* 37.

49. *Asperger Syndrome.* Writer's Corner, 2001.

50. Barkley, *Taking Charge of ADHD,* 200.

51. Russell Barkley, cited in J. Baird, J. C. Stevenson and D. C. Williams, "The Evolution of ADHD: A Disorder of Communication?" *Quarterly Review Biology* 75, no. 1 (March 2000): 17-35.

52. Simon, *What Is Attention Deficit Disorder?*
53. *Journal of American Academy of Child and Adolescent Psychiatry* 35, no. 9 (1996): 1193-204, cited in *ADD and ODD Oppositional Defiant Disorder, Attention Deficit Disorder.* Found at http://www.add.miningco.com. 31 May 2001.
54. American Psychiatric Association, *Diagnostic and Statistical Manual,* 92.
55. "Explosive Children." Found at http:// www.Oprah.com. February 2000.
56. Geoffrey Cowley, "Understanding Autism," *Newsweek,* 31 July 2000, 6.
57. Arthur L. Robin, *ADHD in Adolescents* (New York: Guilford Press, 1998), 207.
58. Ross W. Greene, *The Explosive Child* (New York: HarperCollins, 1998), 90.
59. Greene, *The Explosive Child,* 90.
60. A summary of what they've said in their works throughout the years.
61. Wing, *The Autistic Spectrum: A Parent's Guide,* 37.
62. Leo Kanner, "Autistic Disturbances of Affective Contact," *Nervous Child* 2 (1943): 217.
63. Kanner, "Autistic Disturbances of Affective Contact," 245.
64. Harvey Simon, M.D., *What Is Attention Deficit Disorder?* Found at CBS Health-Watch. http://www.cbshealthwatch.medscape.com. 6 January 2001. 4.
65. Temple Grandin, *Thinking in Pictures* (New York: Doubleday, 1995), 68.
66. Simon, *What Is Attention Deficit Disorder?*

Chapter 4—The Problem with Current Diagnostic Practices

1. National Institute of Health, *NIH Consensus Panel Statement Cites Inconsistencies in Care for Children with ADHD.* Found at http://dowland.cit.nih.gov/odp/consensus/news/releases/110_release.htm. 3 January 2001.
2. American Academy of Pediatrics, *Clinical Practice Guideline: Diagnosis and Evaluation of the Child with ADHD,* 2000, 2.
3. American Academy of Pediatrics, *Clinical Practice Guideline,* 2.
4. *Diagnostic Options in Autism: A Guide for Professionals.* Found at http://www.oneworld.com. 2000.

5. American Academy of Pediatrics, *Clinical Practice Guideline: Diagnosis and Evaluation of the Child with Attention Deficit/Hyperactivity Disorder* 105, no. 5 (2000): 8.
6. American Academy of Neurology and the Child Neurology Society, "Practice Parameter: Screening and Diagnosis of Autism," *Neurology* 55 (2000): 468.
7. Diane Twachtman-Cullen, *Traversing the Autistic Continuum: Meeting the Challenges* (workshop at Indiana University, Bloomington, Ind., 1997), 1.
8. American Academy of Pediatrics, *Clinical Practice Guideline,* 10.
9. Stephanie Brush, "Pay Attention," *USA Today,* 13-15 July 2001, sec. Weekend, 6-7.
10. National Institute of Mental Health, *Interdisciplinary Research on Attention Deficit Hyperactivity Disorder* (Washington, D.C., 2000).
11. National Institute of Mental Health, *Interdisciplinary Research.*
12. If you are interested in participating or know an eligible family, please call to discuss the details of the study: Dr. Donna Spiker, Stanford University, (650) 723-7809, spiker@stanford.edu. You may also write to Stanford Autism Research Program, Dept. of Psychiatry, Mail Code 5719–401 Quarry Road, Stanford University, Stanford, CA 94305-5719.
13. Research Units on Pediatric Psychopharmacology (RUPP) are research project sites funded by the National Institutes of Mental Health. Five RUPP-Autism sites in locations throughout the United States are conducting studies on various disorders.
14. The Collaborative Autism Project (CAP) is a joint project between Tufts University/New England Medical Center, The University of Iowa, Johns Hopkins, and Vanderbilt University to search for the genes that may cause autism. Dr. Susan Folstein is the Principal Investigator at the New England Medical Center Site. If you are interested in participating or would like more information, please contact Raphael Bernier or Sarah Svenson. E-mail: raphael.bernier@es.nemc.org
15. Duke University Center for Human Genetics. Contact: autism_mail@chg.mc.duke.edu.

16. Yale Child Study Center, Yale University School of Medicine, 230 S. Frontage Road, P.O. Box 207900, New Haven, CT 06502. (203) 785-2510. Web site: http://info.med.yale.edu/chldstdy/autism
17. For more information on this study, please contact: Dr. Eric Hollander, Clinical Director, Seaver Center, Mount Sinai School of Medicine, New York, NY. (212) 241-2994. E-mail: E_Hollander@smtplink.mssm.edu
18. National Institute of Mental Health, *Brain Gene Implicated in Autism* (2001): 1.
19. J. Piven et al., "Broader Autism Phenotype: Evidence from a Family History Study of Multiple-Incidence Autism Families," *American Journal of Psychiatry* 154, no. 2 (1997): 185-90.
20. Ed Cook, "Autism: Review of Neurochemical Investigation," *Synapse* 6, no. 3 (1990): 292-308.
21. National Institute of Mental Health, "Brain Gene Implicated in Autism," 1.
22. Families for Effective Autism Treatment, "Strong Evidence for Linkage to Chromosomes 2q, 7q, and 16p," *American Journal of Human Genetics* (2000): 1.
23. "Healing Autism: No Finer a Cause on the Planet," *Feat Daily Newsletter,* Sacramento, Calif. Found at http://www.feat.org. 1999.
24. "Healing Autism: No Finer a Cause."
25. Mark Wolraich, "Attention Deficit Hyperactivity Disorder: Current Diagnosis and Treatment," (American Academy of Pediatrics Annual Meeting, Chicago, Ill., 29 October 2000), 4.
26. Jill Evancoe, Betsy Harman, and Jason Inman, *What Causes Autism, Attention-Deficit Hyperactivity Disorder, & Bipolar Disorder? Broadening the Public's Knowledge Through an Interactive Molecular and Genetic Investigation* (Harrisonburg, Va.: James Madison University, 1999).
27. Mark D. Rapport, M.D., "Bridging Theory and Practice: Conceptual Understanding of Treatments for Children with Attention Deficit Hyperactivity Disorder (ADHD), Obsessive-Compulsive Disorder (OCD), Autism, and Depression," *Journal of Clinical Child Psychology* 30, no. 1 (2001): 3-7.

28. E. Schopler, R. J. Reichler, and B. R. Renner, *Childhood Autism Rating Scale* (Los Angeles: Western Psychological Services, 1988).
29. C. K. Conners, *Conners' Rating Scale Manual* (North Tonawanda, N.Y.: Multi-Health Systems, Inc., 1989).
30. T. Achenbach, *Child Behavior Checklist* (Burlington, Vt.: University of Vermont, 1991).
31. Stephen Ehlers, Christopher Gillberg, and Lorna Wing, "A Screening Questionnaire for Asperger Syndrome and Other High-Functioning Autism Spectrum Disorders in School Age Children," *Journal of Autism and Developmental Disorders* 29, no. 2 (1999): 129-41.

Chapter 5—The Changing Faces of Autism

1. Stanley I. Greenspan and Serena Weider, *The Child with Special Needs* (Reading, Mass.: Merloyd Lawrence, 1998).

Chapter 6—Careers and Relationships

1. R. Peter Hobson, quoted in Steve Gutstein, *My Baby Can't Dance* (1999), 1. Found at http://www.connectionscenter.com
2. Tony Attwood, *Conference 2000 Tony Attwood Lecture Outline.* Found at http://www.faaas.org. 24 May 2001.
3. Liz Seymour, *Condition Bears Gifts, Frustrations.* Found at http://washingtonpost.com. 7 August 2000.
4. Lawrence Osborne, "The Little Professor Syndrome," *New York Times Magazine,* 18 June 2000.
5. Attwood, *Conference 2000.*
6. John Ratey, "The Biology of ADD," (First Annual National ADDA Adult ADD Conference, Merrillville, Ind., 20-22 April 1995).
7. Edward M. Hallowell and John J. Ratey, *Driven to Distraction* (New York: Pantheon, 1994), 73-6.

8. Attwood, *Conference 2000.*
9. Hallowell and Ratey, *Driven to Distraction*, 110-7.
10. Attwood, *Conference 2000.*
11. Families of Adults Afflicted with Asperger's Syndrome, *Clinical Characteristics of Mild Autism in Adults*. Found at http://www.faaas.org, 5. 1994.
12. Ratey, "The Biology of ADD."
13. Digby Tantun, quoted in Ami Klin, Fred R. Volkmar, and Sara S., eds. Sparrow, *Asperger Syndrome* (New York: Guilford Press, 2000), 392.

Chapter 7—Treatments for ADHD and Autism

1. Polly A. Yarnell, *Autism Workshops and Seminars* (Ceres, Calif.: Autism Consultancy Services, 1999), 4.
2. Lorna Wing, *The Autistic Spectrum: A Guide for Parents and Professionals* (London: Constable and Company, 1997).
3. B. J. Freeman, "The Advocate Interview," *The Advocate Newsletter of the Autism Society of America* (fall 1993): 8.
4. Lynn Hamilton, *Facing Autism* (Colorado Springs, Colo.: WaterBrook, 2000), 81.
5. Hamilton, *Facing Autism,* 81.
6. Ivar Lovaas, quoted in Hamilton, *Facing Autism,* 83.
7. Stanley Greenspan, *Playground Politics* (Reading, Mass.: Perseus, 1993), 272.
8. Greenspan, *Playground Politics,* 273.
9. Hamilton, *Facing Autism,* 68.
10. Bernard Rimland, "Advancing the Frontiers of Research: The Defeat Autism Now! Project," (ASA National Conference on Autism, Orlando, Fla., 8-12 July 1997), 177.
11. Stanley Greenspan, *The Child with Special Needs* (Reading, Mass.: Merloyd Lawrence, 1998), 341.

12. Antoinette Lubrano, "Let's Create Beautiful Music Together," *Autism Digest* (May-June 2000): 27.
13. Greenspan, *The Child with Special Needs,* 299.
14. John Ratey, *A User's Guide to the Brain* (New York: Pantheon, 2001), 178.
15. Greenspan, *The Child with Special Needs,* 299.
16. Warren Bruhl, "Pediatric Chiropractic for Developmental Delays," *Developmental Delay Resources* (spring 2000): 7.
17. T. M. Field et al., "Adolescents with Attention Deficit Hyperactivity Disorder Benefit from Massage Therapy," MEDLINE (1998), 1.
18. Matthew Cohen, "Summary of IDEA/Section 504," *ADD and Adolescence* (Washington, D.C.: Children and Adults with Attention Deficit Disorder, 1996), 52-3.
19. Fred Volkmar, *Pharmacological Interventions in Autism: Theoretical and Practical Issues* (abstract, 2001), 80-7.
20. MTA Cooperative Group, "A Fourteen Month Randomized Clinical Trial of Treatment Strategies for Attention-Deficit/Hyperactivity Disorder," *Archives of General Psychiatry* 56 (1999): 1073-86. Found at http://www.ncbi.nlm.nih.gov/entrez/query.fcgi?cmd=Retrieve&db=PubMed&list_ulds=9294378&dopt=Abstract. A search on PubMed (http://www.ncbi.nlm.nih.gov/entrez/query.fcgi) with search terms "ADHD" and "MTA" will reveal a number of articles devoted to this study. Clicking "Related article" also gives more articles.
21. John Scott Werry, "Pharmacological Treatments of Autism, Attention Deficit Hyperactivity Disorder, Oppositional Defiant Disorder, and Depression in Children and Youth," *The Journal of Clinical Child Psychology* 30 (March 2001): 110-3.

Chapter 8—Triumphs

1. Used by permission of The Ned Herrmann Group, Inc., 794 Buffalo Creek Road, Lake Lure, NC 28746.
2. Used by permission of The Ned Herrmann Group, Inc.

3. Used by permission of The Ned Herrmann Group, Inc.

Conclusion—New Beginnings

1. Lorna Wing, quoted in Eric Schopler, Gary B. Mesibov, and Linda Kunce, eds., *Asperger Syndrome or High Functioning Autism?* (New York: Plenum Press, 1998), 25.
2. F. Sara Beth, "Is My Son Normal? One Mother's Journey," *Redbook,* November 1996, 77ff.
3. Larry B. Silver, M.D., *ADHD: Attention Deficit-Hyperactivity Disorder and Learning Disabilities* (Summit, N. J.: Ciba-Geigy Corporation, Pharmaceuticals Division, 1995), 9.

Index